CUBA 18, U.S. 50
MY FIFTY YEAR TRIP

A tribute to family and country

Historical Autobiography

Dr. Rolando M. Ochoa DBA

Published by Eriginal Books LLC
Miami, Florida
www.eriginalbooks.com
www.eriginalbooks.net

Printed in the United States

ISBN 978-1-61370-097-6

TABLE OF CONTENTS

FOREWORD

Rolando Ochoa, the author of this book, was born in Havana, Cuba, in 1943. I was born in Pittsburgh, PA, in 1953, and our lives might, at first, appear to have little in common. Yet they've intersected directly at several points – most significantly in the very last page of this memoir, in which he notes the birth, in 2015, of his granddaughter Reina.

What a coincidence. She's my granddaughter, too.

Another coincidence: On the very same day Rolando and his lovely wife, Yolanda, were attending the wedding of their son Roland, I was attending the wedding of my daughter, Kristin, whose marriage ceremony, in every way, was just as beautiful, festive, original, and memorable as was Roland's. That's because they were marrying one another that day – and our two families became intertwined, from that day forward.

And now, from this day: foreword!

The fact that I've written books, and now am writing a foreword to Rolando's book, hardly surprises me, because, in reading his honest and often astounding account of his family history, I've encountered, time and again, points along the way where our respective life paths have converged, or come very close.

At first, the connections were very remote, or marked by several degrees of separation. My family moved to South Florida in 1960; he and his family arrived, under very different circumstances, in 1962. He worked at the same grocery chain where I later shopped, and eventually lived in Plantation, the neighboring community to my family home in Fort Lauderdale.

But we both attended, and were graduated from, Broward Community College at the same time in the 1970s, before I went on to the University of Florida, and Rolando went on to Nova University – the same institution where my daughter (now his daughter, too) earned her law degree. He earned a doctorate there, and is now, as he'll tell you, a full-time professor. I'm now a full-time professor, too, but without the doctorate.

I teach TV history – and Rolando's life story is a chapter of TV history I had never known before. It's the history of Cuban television, where Rolando's father was the star, for more than a decade, of the top-rated TV show in all of Cuba. And the story of how Rolando himself became a widely recognized and highly paid child TV star there, before Fidel Castro's revolution changed everything.

Rolando's book is a firsthand account of the results of that change of power – a narrative that is told in such a direct and truthful manner, it acknowledges fears and dreams, resentments and achievements with equal candor. As a history of the impact of the Cuban revolution, as well as an unblinking account of one man's life, this book is valuable.

And the photos? They're invaluable. Not only do they attest to the truthfulness of the story Rolando tells here, but they offer a visual record of a Cuban show-business era that's long gone – and that, without this book's publication, might never be so effectively recorded.

David Bianculli, May 2017
TV & Film Professor, Rowan University, NJ
TV Critic, NPR's Fresh Air with Terry Gross

PREFACE

The original idea for this book was conceived on an airplane trip when I felt the need to tell my story, not only to document it for present and future members of my family as a manifesto, but also to tell the world this unusual story that describes many events, both personal and general, that took place during these years from the perspective of a Cuban refugee.

Family data and memories were used to compile the stories as well as conversations with my wife, Yolanda, who is a big part of the story. Yolanda served, not only as a source of validation, but also as sort of censor for the book, as she insisted that the descriptions of the events be told in good taste and respecting privacy.

I want to acknowledge the help of my daughter-in-law Stephanie, who helped me with editing at first, as well as my sister Susy, for her input in all the chapters. There were also two friends to whom I gave part of the manuscript to read: Rene Smith and Jerry Head; one a Cuban and the other an American. I wanted to get feedback as to their opinion and whether or not they considered the content interesting and informative. Both of these friends provided me with invaluable feedback.

My eternal gratitude also goes to Dr. Maria Villar-Smith PhD for her assistance and her expert advice, product of her credentials and ample experience in writing. Dr. Villar-Smith is a full professor in the School of English and my colleague at Miami Dade College.

I hope that the readers of this book enjoy the stories and appreciate its relevance, especially during these times (2015) when the Cuba-US relations are in the negotiation stage and in the forefront of current events. It is my fervent desire that one day, hopefully soon, Cuba and the suffering Cuban people on the island will be totally free and independent, and that they will be able to enjoy the freedoms and rights that we enjoy in the U.S.

Chapter One
Introduction. Family Origins

I do not travel much by air. In fact, I have not done a lot of traveling at all except for the occasional car trip within the southeastern United States. However, when the sun rose today, it found me driving not on my daily commute from my house in Pembroke Pines to my job in Sunny Isles Beach, but to the Miami International Airport (MIA) for the first leg of a business trip that would eventually take me to San Diego, California. It was a cool morning in South Florida, and the roads were practically empty of all the cars and trucks I usually encounter every morning on my 30-mile commute to work. I said to myself: "Wouldn't it be nice to have this kind of traffic every day?" Dreaming is cheap! Those living in or near a large metropolitan area must endure the rigors of traffic congestions, accidents and road repairs on a daily basis with little or no choice in the matter. The best way to go through it is to find something to do with your mind and not get stressed out. Any South Floridian must learn to accept these rigors. It is the price one pays for living "in paradise."

My radio, as is the case every morning, was tuned to my favorite music station. My mind drifted back fifty years ago when, as young man of 18, I arrived at MIA. Many things have happened during these five decades and, only God knew how much I still missed my homeland. With melancholic sadness, my thoughts went back to those days of my early childhood and adolescence in Havana. (The original name of the capital of Cuba is "San Cristobal de La Habana", later, it became "La Habana"). As my mind flooded with the memories, I realized that the music playing on the car radio set the perfect background mood for my thoughts, just like in the movies.

My childhood in Cuba had been an unusual one. I was the first child born to a couple of struggling actors. I also had a sister, Cecilia, from my mother's first marriage to one of Cuba's premier bandleaders and musicians, Raimundo Palau. My father, Rolando Ochoa and Garcia was the son of a pharmacy practitioner, Manuel Ochoa Muro, and grandson of Doctor Guillermito Ochoa, the town's family doctor in Regla, a community located near Havana. My grandmother was Rita Garcia Pujol, a housewife, who descended also from a well-known family in Regla where many of her brothers were veterans of the War of Independence. They had fought and shed their blood to free Cuba from the Spanish totalitarianism. My father had a sister named Rina who was a couple of years older than him. At the age of 16, my father joined the chorus of the famous theater "Teatro Martí de La Habana".

The year was 1932, and the political situation in Cuba was very tense. The island had suffered, as most nations did, from the rigors of the depression of 1929. President Gerardo Machado was rapidly becoming a dictator. The youth groups, as was always the case, were rebelling against him with daily street demonstrations that at times resulted in many being killed or wounded. My grandfather (Abuelo Manuel) feared for the life and safety of my father, so he persuaded the producer of the theatre, Jose Sanchez Arcilla, to hire my father (who had no acting experience or any formal or informal training in the theatre) to be a member of the chorus. At that time, their repertoire consisted mainly of Cuban and Spanish

14

Operettas, called "Zarzuelas," where the chorus did a lot of singing. My father was not very good. In fact, he could not sing a note! The producer agreed to help his good friend, so he took my father off the politically charged streets and taught him the ropes.

My father used to tell an anecdote documenting his singing ability at the time. The musical director of the company was a known musician and composer by the name of Gonzalo Roig, who later became one of Cuba's premier composers. Maestro Roig, whose most famous song "Yours" (Quiereme Mucho) was featured in a 1939 Hollywood movie called "Shipyard Sally," was rehearsing one day with the chorus a new song while playing the piano. Maestro Roig heard some out of tune notes coming from the chorus. He repeated that part of the song several times but it was no improvement. He then decided to ask every member to sing that part of the song by themselves in order to identify the "culprit." Young Rolando knew it was him, so he got very nervous and when it was his turn, the truth came out. Maestro Roig looked over his small glasses toward my father and said: "Rolando, you are a very special case. You are the only person I know who has one male ear and one female." My father got very upset at this public reprimand and wanted to respond, but did not. His singing ability improved considerably after this incident and he attributed his improvement to that embarrassing episode.

My mother, Josefina Berrio Bonnín (Pepa), in contrast, was the middle child of three sisters born to Spanish actors who had decided to stay in Havana after arriving for a performing tour from Spain. Cuba, also referred to as the Pearl of the Antilles, possessed a special enchantment for many foreigners. Many found it difficult to leave the island after spending some time there. Before my grandparents' decision to reside in Cuba, my mother and her sisters, Dolores (Lolita) and Francisca (Paquita), traveled with them on tours through South and Central America. My mother and her sisters were all part of a "company" where they learned the theatrical profession. My Grandfather, Don Jose Berrio Pasoparga, was a dramatic actor, director, producer, and writer. Considered a very handsome "Caballero Español" from Jerez de la Frontera in the province of Andalucia, he had many years of experience and a complete repertoire of dramas and tragedies, which were popular at the time. My grandmother, Coloma Bonnín Bonnín, was a beautiful young actress and singer from the island of Mallorca in Spain. She had a very strong voice and pair of piercing black eyes that could stop traffic.

My parents met at Teatro Marti when he was 16 and she was 20. My father used to tell me that the moment he saw my mother, he fell madly in love with her. The only problem for him was that she did not want anything to do with a 16 year-old with no apparent theatrical talent and no financial stability at all. She also had gotten recently divorced and was not in the mood for romance. She needed to work and take care of her daughter Cecilia, which she did with the help of my grandmother. My grandmother was even more adamant about my father's intentions and told him to get lost several times, but my father persisted. According to my father, he always knew she was the only one for him.

One day after rehearsals my mother was not feeling well because she had a headache. My father volunteered to give her a forehead massage. The rest is history. They began a romantic relationship and got married. They joined their salaries and with my mother's shrewd administration were able to survive month by month. After several years, I was born in

Havana on November 8, 1943 at a small hospital called "Clínica La Bondad" located at 1263 "Calzada del Cerro" which was considered at the time to be the best in the country. I weighed 8 pounds and 8 ounces, and the week that I was born, the lottery numbers called "terminales" turn out t be 808. These were the last three numbers of the winning number of Cuban Lottery that you could play using the illegal gambling activity called Bolita. My father and many of his friends won some money. Since then, "8" has been my lucky number.

Because they had to work more on the weekends, they used to take me to stay with my aunt Rina Ochoa de Arango, who lived in the nearby beach-town named Cojimar. My aunt was married to Octavio Arango, a construction contractor and real estate investor. They also had a son named Octavio, but everyone called him "Tavito." Tavito was 5 years older and was like a big brother to me. It was not easy to take me to Cojimar every Friday. My parents would take a very small boat called "Lanchita" that crossed the Havana Harbor from a pier in Old Havana to a coastal town named Casablanca. From Casablanca they would take a very short ride in a very short train (maybe one car and the locomotive) to Cojimar. My aunt Rina, would be waiting at the station to receive the "package" and my parents would not even detrain. The trip back to Casablanca would immediately depart after arriving. I usually would stay the weekend with the Arangos and on Monday, the process was reversed. I have some very fond memories of those weekends with family and of my relationship with them.

My entire early life was impregnated with the sounds, terminology, stories, and the romanticism of the world of the theatre and entertainment. At the age of 8, I started what was to be a short, but very successful performing career, as a child actor. Never in my wildest dreams could I have imagined how my life would change in the years to come.

Chapter Two
Trip to San Diego.
Our life changed after 1959

As I approached Miami International Airport, I realized how fast I had made the trip. I began to think about all those activities that travelers face; where to park, check in my baggage, etc. Parking was relatively easy. I thought because it was early Sunday morning, and that not many people travel at that time, it would all go smoothly, but when I got to the ticket counter area, I was surprised to see a very long line of travelers twisting around in a rope system similar to that found at Disney World in Orlando. It was a little after 6:00 AM, and I was concerned that I might not get through the maze in time; I still had to go through the security screening before I could catch my flight to Chicago. However, Flight 417 was only the first leg of the trip.

I patiently waited in line or "cola" (Colas in Spanish also mean tails. I guess the lines were long like monkey tails). Waiting in line is not a pleasant experience for anybody, but most of us know that standing in lines is common anywhere we go. I usually, in fact, do not mind waiting in line too much, except when it is at a restaurant or at a supermarket checkout. I have tried to understand why I only mind waiting in food-related situations. I have always wondered why a line related to food bothers me more than any other. Perhaps my "food line phobia" can be traced back to those stressful and inexplicable food lines called "colas." Those interminable lines were a part of life in Fidel Castro's Cuba. These "colas" appeared in my troubled island right after January 1, 1959, when it was taken over by, in my opinion, the worst dictator that has ever lived, Fidel Castro.

The Cuba where I grew up was a very complex society. There were military takeovers, revolutions, many crooked politicians who stole from the people, American mafia influences and many other problems, but there was never a shortage of food until this bearded, incompetent, liar, murderer, egotistical, and vengeful criminal took over our island. Under the pretense of being a liberator and a peace-seeking believer in democracy, he fooled many of us. There were of course poor people in Cuba before Castro's arrival, but there were no shortages of food or food lines. Poor people, for the most part, had food and they had the freedom to choose how they wanted to live their lives. There were, like in any society, some abuses and some discrimination, but for the most part, Cubans were free to choose.

My parents were a good example of this. They had both come from a very modest background. After they were married and living on their own, they barely made $1.50 per day combined; this was considered below average income in 1935 Cuba. Even back in early 1930's Cuba, they had the freedom to work hard. They took chances and made opportunities for themselves in order to prosper and enjoy the fruits of their labor. At one time my father held three jobs: In the mornings and evenings he worked at CMQ Radio and TV, and in the afternoons as its Masters of Ceremonies and comedian at Teatro America, and evenings until 3 AM he was the Masters of Ceremonies of one the best night clubs in Havana called: Sans Souci. He paid his dues in abundance!

My father had already risen to stardom when Fidel Castro forced President Batista out of office with the help of the United States government (Bonachea & San Martin, 1974), he was at the top of his career. He was the star of the show with the highest ratings on TV named "Casino de la Alegría." My mother had also placed herself among the best TV actresses of the time with her very famous role in the sitcom called "Familia Pilon." She played a tender yet strong character, the matriarch of a family. Both of them, with hard work, dedication, and high professional standards, enjoyed a very comfortable life by 1958. The "middle class" in Cuba, such as my family, was the largest sociological group, and most of them had gotten there by the freedom to choose and their hard work. They were not part of any oligarchy as they were at one point later accused of being by the revolution's leaders. They were peace loving people who worked hard and lived their lives the best they could without trying to control anyone or hurt anyone.

Having such wonderful professional and personal success, my parents were able to offer my three sisters and me a very comfortable life, and even though we were not considered rich, we had everything we needed. Between both of their base salaries they made around $6,000 a month (In today's dollars it would be around $50,000 per month at a 3.65% inflation rate. The Cuban Peso was at par with the U.S. Dollar at the time). Coming from a humble background, both of my parents were not extravagant with their spending. My mother was more conservative than my father, and she maintained control of the family finances. My father was a care-free person who did not put that much value on money itself. What he valued was his successful career and the ability to provide well for his family. My mother was the daughter of immigrants and had endured the rigors of life that taught her to save instead of spend. She was a great administrator while my father provided most of the funds. It made for a great combination!

My father was ahead of his time in his approach to what was important in life. He was probably the only big-name star in Cuba who when his yearly contract at CMQ TV was to be negotiated for renewal, would go to the head of the station, Goar Mestre, and tell him that he did not want a raise, but wanted to work less for the same amount of money. Year after year he was able to negotiate his contract down to only one TV show per week. This TV show was rated #1 in all of Cuba for the last 11 years before the God-awful revolution era that destroyed Cuba and put a knife into the heart of every freedom loving Cuban.

My father would then spend the rest of his time with his family and enjoying Boca Ciega beach. After many years living in Havana, my parents bought a home in Boca Ciega, so we could go there on weekends and in the summer. This was a wonderful place to raise a family. It was not really large, but it was a gated community where only residents and approved guests could enter. The water and sand on the beach were fantastic and there were many families like ours that made this community feel like one large family where everyone knew everyone else.

Boca Ciega is located about half an hour east of Havana by way of "La Vía Blanca" (The White Way). You can get there by taking the Havana Harbor Tunnel. A Frenchman, Juan Hidalgo, who had a vision, did the development of Boca Ciega. He started selling parcels of an area mostly composed of marshes near a small river. My parents were introduced to this small "paradise" by my Uncle Dr. Alberto Barba Inclan who was married to Aunt Paquita. My aunt and uncle built their summer house there. They would go on the weekends and stay longer in the summer with their two children my dear cousins Lucrecia (Luqui) and Ernesto. My Uncle Alberto was a renowned orthopedic surgeon in Havana and my aunt, Paquita was his assistant and physical therapist. They had also worked very hard. He practiced out of his home, and he was on the staff of "Clínica Cardona." Additionally, he was a Major/Doctor for the National Police and worked in the "Hospital de La Policía." (Hospital for the Police) Uncle Alberto came from a famous medical family. Among his relatives was Dr. Clemente Inclán, his uncle and the rector of the University of Havana, he himself an excellent pediatrician. Dr. Clemente was also my pediatrician.

In Boca Ciega the river would flow during the rainy season, but its mouth would close when the northern winds attacked the Cuban coast. The name Boca Ciega means Blind Mouth in English, probably named so because once the mouth of the river closed, the river actually became a lake for a few months each year. The rains would return, and the "lake" would overflow, making its mouth open wide again. Some years the mouth had to be artificially opened by a bulldozer in order to prevent flooding in the streets and homes.

Around 1953, my parents made the decision to move to Boca Ciega full-time, and we were one of a few families that lived there year-round. The house was remodeled and a second floor was added with three bedrooms and a bathroom. Fortunately our school in Havana, "Colegio Cubano Arturo Montori," had a bus route that picked us up at 6:00 AM, then picked up other students at many of the other beaches along the way to Havana. We usually got to school around 8:00 AM. I guess I was a product of "busing" many years before it became a household term coined during the civil rights movement in the U.S. The process would be repeated in reverse in the afternoon five days per week. During the trip back, I would do all my homework. To this day I think that the reason my handwriting is so bad is because of the jerking movement of the bus, as I tried doing my homework. At least that is my story, and I am sticking to it.

Boca Ciega was great in the summer and also on the weekends when more people came, but the rest of the time, it was really too slow for me. It was like living in a remote area or a desert. I wrote a poem describing how I felt at the time titled; "Soneto a Boca Ciega:"

Vivo yo en lugar
Tan bonito como fresco
A veces yo lo detesto
Tanto como El Viejo al Mar

Uno sale a pasear
Y empieza a oír un concierto
De grillos en el manglar

Esta es mi playa-desierto
Donde uno tiene que hablar
Y hasta jugar con los muertos

English Translation:

I live in this pretty and cool place,
But sometimes I hate it as the old man did the sea

One goes for a walk and starts to hear a concert
Of grasshoppers in the mangroves
This is my beach/desert where you have to talk
And even play with the dead.

The pleasure that I experienced when all my friends and their families showed up was the payoff, and more than made up for all the boring times. My Dad loved it! He had a few close friends and they would take long walks in the sand, would go to lunch at the local "bodega," and at night would play dominos in the back porch at the Frenchman's house.

I also had many friends and a few very close friends, who played sports together, rode motorcycles, rode horses, and were inseparable. Most of them continue to be my close friends, and we see each other very often for lunch or other activities. This friendship of over 60 years is a wonderful thing to have so I want to thank: Severo Rodriguez, Julio Diaz, Siro del Castillo, and Alberto Guernica for their friendship and support then, in Cuba, and now in the U.S.

To keep my sister, Pepita, and I entertained, my parents bought us horses. My first horse was named Niño (Boy), a palomino gelding, yellow with a white mane. Pepita's horse was named Niña (Girl), a Trinitarian pinto pony with several colors. We did not give them these names; they came with the names already. At first we did not have a stable to keep them in, so they were tied up to a stake on an empty lot with plenty of grass. We would give them their daily rations of corn and corn meal, plus plenty of water. There was this worker named Tápanes, who would take care of the horses and taught us a lot about them. We would saddle them and ride all over the place. Several of my friends also had horses, and we would ride together and invent games with them. We would even take them to the beach and make them swim when the sea was calm. Both my sister and I became very good riders for our ages.

One year, for my 11th birthday my parents bought me a second horse. This horse was very tall, a sorrel stallion with a lot of vigor and very difficult to ride. His name was Caramelo (Butterscotch Candy), and I needed a bench to reach the stirrup to mount him. By this time someone had built a stable and all three horses lived there. Caramelo was very much in love with any mare that was remotely close to him. When that happened, it was very hard to handle him, and even though I learned to do it, and he obeyed my commands, I was not having a good time. I was too busy handling Caramelo to enjoy my friends, our games, and the whole idea of riding for fun. One day I went to my dad and I asked him to sell Caramelo because I wanted to go back and ride good old Niño again. He understood and sold it back to the friend who had sold it to him. I was relieved.

All the children of the families that lived in Boca Ciega, my hometown, had a great time there. Many of us had horses. Many of them had also motorcycles, bicycles, and played a lot of sports. We had a small clubhouse with a basketball court, a playground, and pool and Ping-Pong tables. We also played dominos, canasta, and in the summer, evening dances were organized. Every summer in August we would have the big "Verbena." It was like a fair with amusement rides, and on the last night, there would be a really big dance party. My dad was the president of the club, and with his connections, he would bring big name bands from Havana to play. We had among others: Orquesta Aragon, Fajardo y sus Estrellas, Orquesta Anacaona, and one year the great Beny Moré y su orquesta. As a young man, I would always relish these times and the clean and safe fun we all had in Boca Ciega.

In the summer we had an intra-club softball league, which was composed of four teams. The teams were named very appropriately: Piratas (Pirates), Tiburones (Sharks), Pulpos (Octupuses), and Cangrejos (Crabs). My father was the pitcher of "Los Cangrejos" and I was his catcher. We hired umpires and we had someone keep score. Every Saturday we would play a double-header and we had lots of fun and many fans came to see and cheer for their team. It was clean fun among friends and neighbors. It was not without the occasional controversy and heated discussions; however, that traditionally characterizes Cubans in general.

Interestingly, I was not a very good student and I had major problems during the Fifth Grade. I had flunked Orthography and Calligraphy and had to go to summer school. I went to summer school, and with a lot of effort, passed both of these "hideous" subjects. It happened that during that particular summer a few of my friends had gotten motorcycles. I wanted one too, so I went to my dad, not my mom because I knew that with her I had a "no" to start with. When I asked my dad, he laughed and said: "Motorcycle for you? Motorcycles are for boys who are good students and do not need to go to summer school." I left very disappointed, but later came up with a plan to get my motorcycle. I went to my dad and asked him if I would get all A's in sixth grade, would he buy me a motorcycle. My dad who was always humoring everything said: "If you, the student who could not pass fifth grade can get all A's in sixth grade, one of the hardest grades, I would buy you one." Later when he told my mom, she almost killed him. He told her that he was 100% sure that I would not get all A's, so they were safe.

Sixth grade came and went and this terrible student got all A's and a few awards also. My dad was mad at me because he told me that I was not a bad student, but a lazy one. My mom was so mad at my dad and told him not to buy it, but my dad told her that he had given his word and he was going to buy it. I got my motorcycle. It was a used BSA 125 cc that did not go very fast, but it was good enough for me. I also got a list of rules and regulations as to what I was permitted to do with the motorcycle. You will not speed, you will not do tricks, you will not ride outside of the limits of Boca Ciega, and you will not ride with a passenger. I have to say that I did not follow any of these rules. I was careful, and for many years I used it without any accidents. It was not until 1959 when I was nearly 16 that I suffered my first accident.

I was going to Havana (which was off limits) to visit my girlfriend. As I pulled out of the Havana Bay tunnel and headed into Malecón Street: it had started to rain really bad. I then turned into one of the narrow streets of "La Habana Vieja" (Old Havana) to find somewhere to wait out the rain. As I was approaching an intersection a man came out of nowhere behind a fruit cart and appeared in front of me. I applied the brakes in order to avoid hitting him, and my bike slipped sideways, and I dragged for over 20 feet until I stopped. The bike had considerable damage, and I had my right leg bruised and it was bleeding. Now I was in trouble! I decided to go to the nearby Teatro Nacional (National Theater) where my father was rehearsing and faced up to my mistake. When my father saw my condition and that of the bike, he was pretty mad. This was for sure the maddest I had ever seen him. He told me that I would lose my bike and that he would sell it right away to the first person that made him an offer. So he did. I was grounded for a while and my wounds were mended. I learned a valuable lesson.

My father loved cars. The newest U.S. manufactured cars would be introduced in Cuba at about the same time as in the U.S., and I particularly remember my father loving General Motors cars. He would go to the dealer and buy a new model, even though his car would be just a year old. He would drive it proudly home where he knew my mother was waiting to have a fit and reproach him for his lack of financial responsibility. They sometimes would argue for days about his car-buying escapades. One day I asked my father why he bought the new cars knowing that my mother would fight with him. He then told me that he knew that they could afford a new car, but that if he asked my mother for her opinion, she would have never agreed to it. So he would buy it, put up with a few days of arguments and disagreements, which would eventually end, and everything would go back to normal, and he would keep his new car. His last car in Cuba was a light blue four-door 1959 Chevrolet Bellaire.

Back then food was plentiful and Cuba was self-sufficient in most, if not all, the food needs of the population. The "Red Crowd" that has des-governed Cuba since 1959, also destroyed most of our industries as part of the macabre plan to make everyone equal at the bottom of the socio-economic scale. All the power now rests in the hands of a gang of miscreants and criminals. They killed all the incentive to prosper from Cubans and they have also ruined the entire infrastructure with their incompetence. They indirectly promoted among Cubans a lack of pride in their work and lives.

Standing in a "cola" was one of the most denigrating experiences I remember from those very difficult days of my adolescence. If you get up in the morning, not knowing if you or your family are going to eat that day, you do not have too much time to think about overthrowing the government or starting a counter-revolutionary group. This was and still is a very important and effective part of maintaining the macabre plan.

The fight for survival, made my father buy some chickens so we would always have at least eggs. Soon there was no more feed for the chickens, so I had to find and kill frogs and earth crabs to feed the chickens. The chickens seemed to prefer these two "gourmet" delicacies rather than the feed and corn they were used to eating before. The frogs and crabs were not too happy, but had no say in the matter. My father also asked a friend by the name of Higinio, chief of a fishing crew, to allow me, unofficially, to be part of his government-run fishing crew. Every morning at 4:00 AM Higinio would pick me up at our home in Boca Ciega Beach, and we would go fishing with a very large net called a "chinchorro".

My parents had taken me out of my last year of high school after my private school, Colegio Cubano Arturo Montori, was "nationalized." The owners of the school, as in most other entities nationalized, were Cubans and not foreigners. Therefore, when communists use the term "nationalization" they mean properties and other goods stolen from their rightful owners. Staying in the government-run school meant that I would have been subjected to communist indoctrination and forced to work as a "volunteer" in Cuba's slave farms. My parents thought that this fishing job was not only a way of keeping me busy and away from government indoctrination, but it also would contribute to the survival of our family.

As a "hired" hand, at the age of 17, my job was to be part of the group who pulled the rope at one of the two ends from the beach in order to bring this extremely large net near the shore. The fish were plentiful and of different species. The entire catch was supposed to go to the government, but Higinio allowed me to pick two buckets full of fish every day to take home as unofficial pay. My knowledge of fishing came in handy because I could choose the best fish. My family would then use the fish as currency and bartered with our neighbors for other foods. Our always very well stocked kitchen before

Castro, was always almost bare even despite these clever efforts.

I was not unfamiliar with fishing because I did it as a hobby while growing up in Boca Ciega Beach, one of the best spots in the northern coast of Havana province. However, one thing was to do it as hobby and another as a job, but I actually liked it because it made me useful and kept me busy. I had learned from my parents the value of work and of doing the best you can no matter what. My adolescence was in stark contrast to my earlier years.

At the age of eight I had my professional acting debut in a radio program with my dad, and at age ten, I was the protagonist in a full-length movie called "Ángeles de la Calle" (Angels of the Street). This movie was filmed in Cuba as a joint venture between a Cuban and a Mexican production company. In 1952 I was signed to an exclusive 2-year contract by U.S. Royal Company, the makers of tires and tennis shoes (Keds). In addition, I was the child star of a musical variety TV show called "Desfile Musical" (Musical Parade). On the show that aired in primetime (Sundays at 8:00 PM) on Channel 6 (CMQ TV) I would perform a musical number plus do all the commercials. For this contract I was paid $500.00 per month and the money went all into a savings account in my name. This was very good money in 1952. In today's dollars at an average inflation rate of 3.65%, it would be over $4,000 per month. Not bad for a ten-year-old kid!

When I was almost 12 years old, the government of Batista through his Minister of Education, Juan Basconcelos, passed a law, forbidding children under 14 to work on television. This halted my career when I was near its top. It is difficult to realize that one can peak at 12 years old. I would not work in television again until I was 15 when I was given a supporting part on a revolutionary television soap opera called: "Juventud en Peligro" (Youth in Danger). There I played a revolutionary who was actually a spy for the Batista government. This soap opera was based on a story of the revolution against Batista. Given that I had the part of a spy, there were times when I had to speak ill of Castro, something I did with great pleasure.

During those years, my parents provided me with a lot of training for my acting career. I took lessons in music, voice, French, ballet, and modern dance, so I would be ready for a career in show business. They hoped I would continue the success that I had as a child star, as a young adult. In the meantime I continued performing on different TV programs and theatrical presentations.

Getting paid in "fish" in 1962 was a far cry from what I had been used to, but it helped me learn many important lessons that would help me for the road ahead. The day we received the telegram announcing that we had been approved to leave Cuba, I was coming back from my job of fishing. My father drove toward the place where I was and found Higinio and me, on the way back. When my father saw us, he started honking for us to stop and I jumped in his car. He was extremely excited, in a way I had never seen him before. He then told me that we were leaving Cuba very soon. It was one of those moments in my life that I will never forget. What would the future bring for us?

Chapter Three
Difficult Decision

W hile standing in line at the airport in Miami (MIA), thoughts of the last day in Cuba came to my mind. That was a terrible day! We had waited for the permit to leave Cuba for almost a year. The rules at the time were that if you wanted to leave Cuba to the United States, you needed a relative in the United Sates to send a visa "waiver" and then you had to resign your job and wait one year without a job and without the "libreta de racionamiento" or ration book. This was a big decision for my parents.

This was the difficult decision that many Cuban parents had to make. Opting to spend a year without a job, income, rations, leave everything that you had, be subject to harassments from the members of the militia and the Defense Committee, known as "El Comité, " and venture into a foreign country with no money, zero assurances of a job, shelter, or assured survival or you could opt to stay in Cuba and take one of two roads: pretend that you supported the miscreants and be an accomplice to all their "fechorías" (misdeeds) or fight the system and the government and risk your physical liberty or even lose your life. After the debacle of Bay of Pigs on April 17, 1961 caused by a cowardly decision of the U.S government to abandon the brave men of the "Brigada 2506," the decision to leave was more justified.

The more successful your life had been, the harder the decision was. My parents took the option to leave Cuba. They were afraid that the government was going to take away all the children from their parents. Their children's future and freedom were more important than all their professional and personal accomplishments, or all the material things that they had. For our family it was a terrible year that culminated with a terrible day at the airport in Rancho Boyeros near Havana.

My father resigned his job at CMQ-TV and started to perform at "Teatro Nacional" (National Theatre) on a show headed by Leopoldo Fernandez (Trespatines), who was one of the top comedians in Cuba. The show consisted of a comedy play and variety acts. Before and after the show, an American movie would be shown. This show was extremely successful given that it was independent from the government and its contents did not have any pro-government propaganda. Many people seeking relief from the constant state-sponsored activities flocked to the theatre and even cheered when an American symbol was shown in the movies. There my father was able to make some money and at the same time, work with his very good friend Leopoldo. On occasions, I would also participate in small parts in the comedy and in the musical numbers.

This show lasted a short time because the government officials made up a false charge that Leopoldo had made a reference on stage about hanging Castro. The charge was that Leopoldo came out carrying a picture of a horse (Some people called Castro "El Caballo" (The Horse)) and his line was supposed to have been: "Este lo cuelgo yo" which means: "This one I will hang." This was absolutely false. Leopoldo never said that and he was very careful not to say anything remotely political because he knew that Castro's agents were everywhere waiting to find an excuse to shut him down. The show was shut down and one of the last truly excellent independent shows in Havana was finished. Leopoldo later took the exile route and became very successful in the U.S. and Puerto Rico.

My aunt, Lolita Berrio, was already in Miami and she was working for La Voz de Las Americas, a radio station that transmitted messages of freedom to Cuba, sponsored by the United States. Tia Lola, as we called her, was also a great comedian and actress in TV in Cuba and was also my godmother. She had come a few months before with her husband Lazaro Dominguez, a radio and TV musical producer, and her granddaughter Cecilia Dubrocq. My cousin, Tía Lola's daughter, Dolores (Lolita) Lopez, was also already in the U.S..

Tía Lola got all of us the visa waiver and she sent them to us. Our group or "núcleo" consisted of my parents, my two sisters, Josefina (Pepita) and Susana (Susy), my grandmother Coloma, and me. My oldest sister, Cecilia, was already in the United States with her husband, Ruben Tamayo, and their two children, Ruben (Ruby) and Cecilia (Cecilu). The situation of our family was not unusual. This family exodus, little by little, was the norm. Those who came first helped the others and so on. Many people in the U.S. and other countries find it hard to understand our exodus. I was very concerned about my future at the time.

Chapter Four
Why?

I have been asked numerous times by those who are not Cubans why did the first group of Cubans leave their country instead of staying there and working towards a return to democracy and freedom. This question does not have an easy answer because every family and every individual had a different reason and motivation for leaving or staying. I can only speculate as to the reasons my family left, what experiences prompted our departure, and why I have not returned.

A lot has been written about the events that took place in Cuba before and after Castro took over the island. If the reader is not familiar with those events, maybe it would help understanding the rest of this chapter by reading one of many great books which relate these events.

Castro, in my opinion, used reverse psychology to his advantage by manipulating the upper classes. Here is why:

He knew that the highly educated and successful portion of Cubans at the time would be an obstacle to his ultimate plan. These groups also held a great portion of the wealth and were the landowners, entrepreneurs, and industry professionals who had helped make Cuba a very advanced country economically and socially.

He knew that if these groups were forced to leave, they would resist because they had too much to lose. He then promulgated regulations that made it very hard to leave the country with the excuse that the revolution needed all its citizens to be integrated. Many felt that as time would pass, leaving would become harder. --Castro's reverse psychology at is best.

These families would leave on their own and Castro would gain by not encountering their opposition and also by keeping all their possessions.

He jailed anyone who opposed any of his mandates and took away jobs and businesses from those who were considered counter-revolutionaries.

He let the word out that the government was going to take charge of all minor children, and that young adults that did not integrate and adopt the Communists ideology, would not be able to go to school and be educated.

Facing these unbearable circumstances most of these families were faced with the decision to stay or leave. Historically, all the political upheavals prior to Castro's takeover had not lasted but a few years, and then most everyone who left would eventually return. Many thought that this time would not be any different. I remember hearing persons around me say: "How could the United States allow a communist government to be instituted in a country so close to them? The U.S will take him out at anytime. In the meantime I am going to Miami for a few years, and then I will come back to Cuba when it is all over." (Famous last words)

The U.S. was the only country, and still is, that opened its doors to Cuban refugees. For this generosity all Cuban exiles should be forever grateful. This good deed indirectly contributed in perpetuating the problem. It was relatively easy to leave, but this played right into Castro's hands by pushing these very same groups that Castro wanted to get rid of into leaving Cuba. This political maneuver inevitably released the internal pressure that could have caused the overthrowing of Castro's newly installed government.

If Cuba had not been 90 miles away from the U.S., and had it been a country in South America, for example, without the easy access by sea and air to the U.S., most Cubans who left in the early years, would have had to stay; they would have fought, gotten their country back, and in my opinion Cuba would be free today. Many would have died, and many more would have had to suffer prison and persecution, but Castro would have not been able to manage and contain this resistance by the ruling classes and these groups would have taken back their country and brought democracy back to Cuba during the time that Castro's power was not yet consolidated.

In summarizing this opinion:

- Castro used reverse psychology and intimidation
- Cubans wanted to protect their families, especially their children
- Cubans thought that their exile would be short-lived
- The proximity to the U.S. and the conditions there, made the exodus easier

By expressing this opinion, I am not reproaching my parents or any other parents who, thinking they were doing the best for their children, left Cuba for the U.S. Most of them, like mine, left everything they had worked for, their possessions, and their memories to take their children to a safer place. I am not blaming the U.S. either for Cuba's predicament. The U.S. has historically had good intentions. The U.S. is always at the forefront in helping any country in the world when help is needed. Unfortunately after 50+ years of slavery, murder, robbery, and lack of every single human right in Cuba, the reality is that the actions taken or lack thereof, by many families and by the U.S., did not translate into results yielding advantages for Cuba and the Cuban people.

Chapter Five
Two Airports: Miami and Havana

As I approached the beginning of the line at MIA, I looked nervously at my watch and realized that I only had fifty minutes to finish the entire process, or I would miss my plane. There were several Japanese families ahead of me in the line, and they were having a tough time trying to communicate with those handling the passengers. Realizing that their language barrier could possibly prevent me from getting to my plane on time, I started to stress out. I said to myself; "I wish these people would have learned how to speak English before they came to this country." "How stupid can they be?" Then another flashback brought me back to reality and I started to laugh on the inside remembering when those same words, "How stupid can you be? ", were told to me and many other Cuban refugees who, like me, came in the early part of the 1960's to South Florida. Back then a lot of the "natives" (I do not mean the Seminoles or the Miccosukees) were not as friendly as the ones portrayed in the classic TV sitcom, Father Knows Best.

Many times I had felt the hard blow of prejudice and lack of understanding that shook all my inner self. South Florida, and especially Miami, where most Cuban refugees decided to stay, was not what it is today. Many Americans who were not Cubans and called themselves "natives" (Who we now call Native-Americans, back then were called American-Indians), did not quite understand what we Cubans were doing here leading to a lack of compassion. We felt contempt by many. How quickly we forget! Now that I am part of the community, now that those same "natives" (you know what I mean) who have stayed (many left Miami-Dade county) understand us better and respect us more. The emigration of Cuban refugees in the 1960's, consisted mostly of professionals, intellectuals, and businessmen, who have enhanced Miami and produced never before seen economic results in the local community. Now standing in line, I entertained the same thoughts of prejudice and looked down on these "foreigners" at the airport counter just because they did not speak English. A very strong shiver went down my spine and I asked God and these Japanese people for forgiveness in the silence of my heart. I also asked God for discernment to never again think like that so I could contribute in my own way toward the eradication of discrimination from the face of the earth.

In my opinion, everyone who makes the U.S. their home, should speak English because English is the language of this country. I also believe that we all should be free to use any language that we want when we are communicating with others who understand it, if we prefer. It is still a free country. All of us who are fortunate enough to speak more than one language (most people in Europe do) must remember to be courteous when others who do not understand our favorite language are around, and we should switch to English, so they do not think that we are talking bad about them, or are saying something that we do not want them to know. It is a free country, but we should also be civil and have good manners.

Because it was getting close to the hour of departure, the ticket agents began calling those passengers going to Chicago ahead of everybody else with the hope of getting us processed before the plane left. We all ran to the security area after checking in our bags only to find that it was also congested. We were lucky that the lines moved quite fast and that most of the passengers did not have too many carry on items. I finally made it to the plane with a few minutes to spare. I got to me seat, 7A, by the window on the left side of the plane and prepared myself with a short prayer asking for protection during the take off and the trip for me and all my fellow passengers. Their survival was also mine.

The takeoff was uneventful and as we were elevated by the powerful jet engines of the aircraft, I looked out my window and saw the airport. I suddenly remembered that in a similar setting on October 7, 1962, I was also on an airplane flying out of Rancho Boyeros, now called Jose Marti International Airport in Havana. Our family of six had gone through the worst day of our lives. This day was the end of a nightmarish year, since we had requested to emigrate to the U.S.

I remember well the night before we left Cuba. We spent it at my uncle's house in El Vedado, near Havana, where Doctor Alberto Barba Inclán, my uncle, lived with his wife, my Aunt Paquita, and my two cousins, Luqui and Ernesto. We had to do that because our house in Boca Ciega and our other properties were confiscated and had to be given to the government the day before. This was one of the conditions imposed by the Castro government if we wanted to leave the country. Several family members and friends came to say goodbye that afternoon and stayed way into the evening. There were many tears and emotionally-charged moments.

Among the visitors were my fiancée and her family. Yes, I had gotten engaged at age 17 to Miss Angela Perez (Not her real name), a beautiful classmate who also lived in El Vedado. We were a bit too young to be engaged, but a few months back, I had bought a ring and asked her mother for her hand in marriage. Our plan was for me to "reclamarla" (claim her) after I got established in the U.S., and then we would get married in the U.S. We also talked about getting married by proxy and then claim her as my wife, if that was necessary. Little did I know that that night would be the last of many nights, days, and many years before I would see her again.

For me, as an inexperienced young man, leaving his sweetheart behind was very difficult, and when we said our goodbyes with a kiss, both of us had tears in our eyes. We looked at each other with our eyes asking why this was happening. I could not sleep that night, and as I tossed and turned in the little bed that my aunt had placed for me in the top back room of her house, I thought of Angela and also of my future in the U.S. Many questions came to mind and the anxiety level grew as I looked at the moon through the full glass windows of the room facing 21 Street in El Vedado. Would I ever come back to my country? Would I be able to again play my beloved guitar given to me by my mother? Would I be able to see my sweetheart again and kiss her and tell her how much I loved her looking at her beautiful large brown eyes? Would Cuba ever be rid of these traitors?

Morning came and with very limited belongings we rode in a taxi to the airport. There were strict rules as to what and how much a person leaving the country could take with them. One of the rules at the time was that you could only bring 3 of everything. It was called a "muda" or outfit. For example 3 trousers, 3 shirts, 3 pairs of socks, 3 underwear shorts, 3 ties, 3 handkerchiefs, etc.

There was a very cruel joke that Cubans were saying those days about the 3 "mudas." This word means outfit, but it also means female mutes, so the joke went like this: A Cuban goes to the airport to leave Cuba and when they opened his luggage to inspect it, they find three girls inside. The government official tells the Cuban that he cannot take 3 girls in his bag and the Cuban guy says: Why not? The rules say that I can take 3 "mudas" and these girls cannot talk. One thing you have to know about Cubans is that no matter how sad and difficult the circumstances are, they will always make a joke about it. My father was a great example of this, and it was his defense mechanism throughout his life. He loved to tell this joke in order to forget that all his other belongings, that he had worked so hard for were left behind.

As we got to the airport, we entered the inspection area where the officials looked through every bag with a fine tooth comb and found nothing outside the rules. My father had admonished my mother telling her not to try anything funny and by all means not to try to smuggle any jewelry. He told her that if she did, and the official found them, he would divorce her or something worse.

Given the economic position of my parents, they had quite a jewelry collection, and my father came up with a scheme to try to get them out before we left. Someone introduced my father to a member of the diplomatic delegation of an embassy (the country will remain our secret) who would, for $1,000 dollars, take a small box of jewels out of Cuba and give them to us in Miami after we arrived. This was a hard decision because we had to trust these jewels to a perfect stranger who came to our house in Boca Ciega, took the jewels in a small box, collected the $1,000 dollars and disappeared leaving us with not even his name. We could not give him everything, but just the best pieces. There were still some more left and those were the ones my father did not want my mother to try to hide and take with her. A few months after we had arrived in Miami, an unknown individual presented himself in our home in Hialeah. He told us he was from the embassy and gave my father that same small box with all our jewels. An honest person! Go figure!

The routine at the airport was very well known by all of us because we had been getting ready for it for a while. The government officials were going to do everything they could to scare us and make us say something so they could accuse us of being counter-revolutionaries or American spies, and consequently cancel our departure. First they would check the bags and take out anything they considered in excess, and then they would place us in a room with glass walls called "la pecera" (the fishbowl) and leave us there for a long while awaiting the departure. From "la pecera" they would call out the names of those who had some problems or they wanted to further harass. Two "milicianos" (militiamen) came to us and asked us to follow them. One was a skinny little man with a bad case of post juvenile acne and the other was a heavyset woman with pants two sizes too small for her. All six of us looked at each other and my father said; "If they retain me, the rest of you go." But then my mother said; " We all go or we all stay!"

We knew that because of my parents' fame, the officials were going to take extra measures in order to provoke us to complain or say something derogatory toward the government. My father had made us promise that no matter what they did, we would not say or do anything to jeopardize our departure. These two *milicianos* took us to two separate rooms. My mother, my two sisters and my grandmother went with the *miliciana* (militiawoman), and my father and I with the *milicianito* (small miliciaman).

Once we were inside we were asked to totally strip, and we were subjected to a full body search. Yes, all of us, except my 7-year old sister. Even my 60-year-old grandmother was strip-searched. When the milicianito told me to do it, I looked at him for a minute and thought; "I could punch this guy so he will never get up again." But my father saw my face and touched my arm and looked at me and told me with his movie actor's trained eyes: "Don't even think about it!"

After this "wonderful" demonstration of how Castro respects his countrymen's human rights, we were back in "la pecera" to wait some more. Then a voice was heard through the speakers saying; "Rolando Ochoa, preséntese a la oficina." (Rolando Ochoa, come to the office). My parents looked at each other, but they did not have to say it twice. The rule was laid down by my mother and that was that. He left and we all stayed back fearing the worst and hoping for the best. After a few minutes, we saw my father coming back with a big smile on his face. We were all standing there waiting to see why he was smiling. Then he came and told us that all they wanted was his raincoat (similar to the one used by "Colombo" in the famous TV series) that he was carrying, because it was not included in the list of items allowed. This was another form of harassment that all Cubans were subjected to when they were going through this process.

We finally boarded the Pan American Airways flight bound to Miami, Florida, USA. My father and I sat together. He was at the window seat and I was in the aisle seat on the right side of the plane. We did not speak very much, and I could see a gleam of tears in his eyes even though he was smiling. The rest of the family sat in front and in back of us. As the plane started to move I saw the face of my father and back of him through the window the airport terminal disappearing on the distance. I sensed an empty feeling in my soul and asked my father: "¿Papi, regresaremos algún día? " (Daddy, are we ever coming back?). He looked at me with a look that I still have vividly in my mind and said: "No lo sé hijo, pero tú y tus hermanas van a ser libres." (I do not know son, but you and your sisters will be free). Every time I am on an airplane takeoff, I think of my father's words and everything that took place that day. It changed my life forever.

Chapter Six
The Land of Opportunity.
Was I ready?

The plane to San Diego was now approaching the outskirts of Miami Dade County. I could tell it was heading toward the vastness of the Florida Everglades. Looking down, I could see how much Miami and outlying areas have grown. The consistently warm weather and real estate values could account for the growth. South Florida's economy entices people from many parts of the country and from other countries to immigrate and settle here. It was not always this way. Back in 1962 when my father and I set out to find a job, South Florida economic prospects were dim. Although we were willing to do anything, it was hard to find a job.

My father, who could not speak a word of English, was determined to find a job outside of his profession. He said that he was tired of working in the entertainment industry doing the same thing for so many years, and that this fresh start in this new country would be the vehicle by which he might start a new career. Even though I did not agree with him, I kept my opinions to myself. I had always admired my father, but now I felt sorry for him. He had lost every material possession he had worked so hard for during the last 30 years in Cuba. He had left behind his successful career, his job, his assets, his fame, and what was more devastating, his ambition. His self-confidence and self-esteem had plummeted, and even though he did not show it, I knew he was very sad and probably in a state of shock. I still grieve for my father.

The plane to San Diego via Chicago was now cruising at 30,000 feet, and the flight attendants were serving drinks and a very light breakfast. As I sipped my coffee carefully, a great idea came to me. For the first time in my life I felt the need to put my life story in writing. I decided to write a book about my life and my experiences. I would write the book in such a way that, as I recount these life experiences and biographical information, they would derive and flow from my experiences on this trip.

This was going to be a very special trip not only because I was going to obtain very useful information at the conference, but also because this book, that I planned to write, would tell my story interlaced with my family story, in all the historical content events, which befell Cuba from 1959 to my present.

The flight took us through a part of the U.S. that I had never seen. As we proceeded north I encountered the beauty of this Land of Opportunity. I was in awe observing the stillness of the marshes in the Everglades of Florida, the splendor of the mighty Mississippi river and all its tributaries, both bodies of water looked like old rivers carved on the earth aging crust. I witnessed beauty beyond my imagination coupled with the vastness of this great land symbolic of this country's greatness. This new country had heart and goodness harboring all who come here seeking freedom, peace, and the pursuit of happiness. How lucky I felt to be able to enjoy the freedom that I had lost in my country, and how fortunate I now was to be able to work and provide my family with a comfortable home.

Unfortunately during the first few years in my new country work opportunities were very limited for Cuban refugees, and many of us found it difficult to support our families. There were language and cultural barriers, coupled with economic and political factors affecting South Florida in the early 1960s. Given the large influx of Cuban refugees during those days and the economic condition of the area, competition for the few good jobs was intense. I was 18 and I had not finished high school. My father was then 46 and had worked for almost 30 years in one profession. In spite of these difficulties, my father, always showed a smiling face. He knew how to play his part. When certain days were particularly difficult, it was hard to know when he was acting like himself or one of the many famous characters he had created.

I quickly realized that I needed to go back to school and finish high school if I were to obtain any kind of decent job. Back in Cuba I could not finish the last year of "Bachillerato" (The close equivalent to a high school diploma, just much harder), because the Cuban government had stolen my school as they had most businesses in Cuba. I have to confess that I was not the model student, not even back home. I struggled through most of my time in my school (Arturo Montori) because I did not apply myself to my studies.

School to me was something that I needed to go through, but my sights were on a career in the entertainment field. The many subjects that I was forced to take did not have anything to do with my career, so I thought. It was difficult for a young boy who had made the type of money that I did (probably more that the principal of the school) to give the necessary importance and effort to his classes. I had reached the last and fifth year of secondary education barely making passing grades. Secondary education in Cuba was very difficult, and the last two years were not designed for students like me. The curriculum was the same for everyone with no electives.

Arturo Montori had been my school since kindergarten. It was a private non-church affiliated school ran by two generations of the Montori family members dedicated to the education of young Cuban minds, in the principles of high academic achievement, love of God, and love of country. This family was revered by the community and by their alumni. My oldest sister, Cecilia, was one of them and during her tenure at Arturo Montori obtained every conceivable honor at her high school graduation. My sister, Pepita, and my cousins, Lolita, Octavio, Ernesto, and many other members of our extended family had also attended that school. After the takeover by Castro, the Montori family was kicked out of the school that they so bravely had created and maintained for many years. This family, as did many others, lost their business, their life efforts, their dreams, their security, and their reasons to live. In fact, the Castro government took advantage of the confusion created by this horrible revolution, to obtain power over the schools and what was taught in them.

To make things worse and more chaotic, the government named one of the lady janitors principal. This deviant tactic was used by the Castro regime in most industries. They gave command to those who never amounted to anything so these incompetent individuals would be so grateful to the government that they would follow their commands without question. This tactic has since backfired and is partly responsible for the complete failure of the Cuban economy after 1959.

At the end of the fourth year of Bachillerato, I did not pass two of my classes (Physics and Natural Sciences), and I had to "arrastrarlas" (dragging them) to the fifth year. The fifth year, in science, I had four classes: Biology, Advanced Math, Ad-

51

vanced Chemistry, and Advanced Physics. The prospects of me making up the two classes from the previous year and passing the four from the fifth year were not very promising, for at 16 I was fully dedicated to my future career, and my extra curricula activities such as my acting and voice lessons, baseball, and attending many lively parties.

Chapter Seven
My Television Career

I started my television career at the age of 8. In 1951 I got a part in a TV drama called "Tensión en el Canal 6" (Tension on Channel 6). I played a boy who falls down a flight of stairs and his parents (the famous actors Carlos Badias and Eva Vazquez) take him to the hospital. I do not remember the rest of the plot.

My father was the Cuban equivalent of Bob Hope in the U.S. He was a renowned master of ceremonies, an excellent stand-up comedian, and a genius of characterizations. He was the star of a TV show called Casino de la Alegría (Casino of Happiness). This show premiered in 1951: The same year Cuban television started. It ranked first place in viewership ratings until 1961 when my father had to resign in order to leave the country. This show was first entitled "Cabaret Regalías" because it was sponsored by the top brand of Cuban cigarettes called "Regalías el Cuño." Later a new sponsor came in and the name was changed. The format of this live show was presented as a real cabaret or nightclub where my father was the MC. He would also do a comedy sketch of situations and events that would occur in a nightclub. He would act out a different characterization each week. One week he would be a rich sultan or tycoon, on another he would be a "guajiro" (farmer) coming to the capital city for the first time. He even had a character who was a Mexican singer!

One day while rehearsing at home in the mirror lip syncing a song by the famous Mexican singer, Pedro Infante, called "Mi Chorro de Voz," (My voice is like a strong jet of water), I stood behind him watching him. I started mimicking him and lip syncing the song quite well. He saw me then turned around and asked me if I wanted to do it instead of him, and I said yes. My father then called the writer of the show named Francisco Vergara, and asked him to change the script to include me. My father's idea was for him to appear first dressed with the typical "Charro" outfit, then a smoke screen would come and as the smoke disappeared I would be there, dressed the same way with a mustache and hat. After being shrunk by the smoke, I would lip sync the song.

The performance caused an enormous positive reaction, not only to the live audience in the studio, but also the next day every major newspaper was talking about it and my father started doing interviews. I became an overnight sensation and then became a regular on the show. I did many other characterizations such as Figaro, The Sad Clown, Danny Kaye, Bola de Nieve and many more. One week my sister, Pepita, who was only 5 years old at the time, joined me in representing a Spanish duet of "El Hijo de Nadie" (No one's son). This presentation was a big success, and my sister and I did a few performances together.

Along with my acting I was also taking different classes such as acting, singing, dancing, fencing, and even French. My parents believed they were priming me for a long-lasting and successful career in show business. They saw in my own career a continuation of their own. All these factors, plus my own laziness toward schoolwork, contributed to my poor performance as a student. My parents expected me to graduate but never applied the pressure that my classmates' parents did for their children to perform well in school. When the school was taken over by the government, I was immediately removed. To this day the question remains if I would have graduated or not. I will never know. Now in the U.S. there was no question in my mind that I needed to finish high school in order to get even the simplest of jobs. My career in show business would have to wait.

Chapter Eight
Living in Hialeah. My First Jobs

We were living in Hialeah, Florida a city north of Miami. A very good friend of my Aunt Lolita had an empty house on the east side, and Lolita had arranged for us to live in the house free of charge. I enrolled in Hialeah Senior High School to get my high school diploma. I was able to bring the grade certificates from my secondary education in Cuba, and thankfully the new school accepted a lot of my credits toward the diploma.

My advisor told me that I needed four classes to graduate: American History, American Government, English Literature, and English Composition. The year had already started in October when I enrolled. Since I could speak, read, and write in English rather well because my school in Cuba had been bilingual, I was placed in the regular classes as a junior, and assigned these classes except for the English Composition which I had to take the following year at night. Many Cubans, who arrived in Miami at the time and attended high school, were placed in remedial English classes first and then transferred into the regular classes, after they had obtained the necessary proficiency in the language. I was fortunate enough to have had previous instruction in English.

My schedule required I take a total of six classes, so I had to choose three more classes as electives. I chose Biology, Physical Education and Trigonometry. The counselor was surprised by my choices, but I wanted to be challenged. Besides, I wanted to also try out for the baseball team by attending physical education, and I was fairly good at math and science at those introductory levels. After the first semester once I found out the school had a choir, I switched Trigonometry for Chorus. I wanted to see if I could introduce myself as a singer given my training.

During Physical Education classes we used to play baseball. I had always played baseball as a child and as a young adult, both in my school's teams and the ones in Boca Ciega. Baseball was and still is one of my favorite sport activities. As a boy of 12 I dreamed of becoming a professional baseball player. This dream was very common in Cuba because Cubans had, and still have an obsession with baseball. If you were a boy and did not or could not play baseball, you were considered an outcast. Boys who could not play baseball had a difficult time with their peers. In my case, I loved it, and I was pretty good at it as well.

When I was a small child my father, who was also a great baseball fan, used to take me at least twice per week, to the "Estadio del Cerro" (Cerro's Stadium) to see the four Cuban League professional teams play. The teams were recognized, not only by their names, but also by their emblems that were animals and by the colors of their uniforms:

- Los Leones de La Habana (The Havana Lions) wore Red
- Los Alacranes del Almendares (Almendares Scorpions) wore Blue
- Los Tigres del Marianao (Marianao Tigers) wore Orange
- Los Elefantes de Cienfuegos (Cienfuegos' Elephants) wore Green

My father and I were fans of the Lions with their red uniforms. Havana and Almendares were the "Eternal Rivals" and most of the time one of these two would win the championship. Many big-league baseball players in the U.S. would go to Cuba to play winter baseball when the season ended in the U.S.. These American players, plus all the great talent in Cuba made this Cuban league a very strong one, and many of the Cuban players would later go on to the big-leagues in America.

Back in Cuba as soon as I became eligible, I played for my school in the inter-collegiate league. I started with 13 year old and younger team, and then I moved to 15 and finally 18. My school had a pretty good team despite being a small school and we competed well every year. I used to play catcher and then I was transferred to first base. At the same time I was also playing in Boca Ciega in what was called "Liga de la Arena del Este" (Eastern Sand League). This league was composed of teams from all the beach developments east of Havana. Boca Ciega a was small community, but we competed in most sports. The coaches were the parents, and each player would buy his own uniform and equipment. My father was the assistant baseball coach, while the baseball manager was our unforgettable, Julio Diaz Rouselot. At the time, in baseball there were very few switch hitters (These are players that can hit both right and left hand). I had developed the ability to be a switch hitter when I was 12, and that gave me an added advantage and improved my batting average a lot.

Back then Cuba also had a team in the Triple "A" minor league of the U.S. which was called the International League. The name of the team was the Cuban Sugar Kings, and my father and I used to go to those games as well. A friend of my father named Bobby Maduro owned the team. Mr. Maduro came up with the idea of using me as the mascot or celebrity guest for the team. Given my father's popularity and also my recent success in television and movies, Maduro thought that I could bring additional attention to the team. My father agreed and I was thrilled.

For a young baseball fan with dreams of becoming a baseball player, being in the dugout with all the stars who I admired so much, learning more about the game, was an unforgettable experience. I was asked to come out between innings so the fans could see me, and I took part in the ceremonies at the beginning of the game, such as throwing the first pitch and other duties. I would also run to deliver the jacket to the pitcher in the event that he would get on base. I learned a lot about the game especially from a veteran pitcher, Julio "Jikí" Moreno. Jikí did not pitch much anymore, and he would sit with me and explain plays and manager's decisions. He became a very good friend and my mentor.

Before the 1959 season, the manager for the Cuban Sugar Kings at the time was Napoleon Reyes, a great player himself. He had been a big-leaguer with the New York Giants. Mr. Reyes invited me to their training camp to try out for a spot in their amateur team. At that time I was 15 years old, six feet tall, and looked older than my actual age. I was in that camp for a very short time. As you know, 1959 was the beginning of the Castro Regime, and one of the actions that the government took was to "nationalize" baseball and stole the teams from the rightful owners. After that all the players and coaches played for the Revolution. The moment that happened, my father took me out the training camp. I cried like a baby and begged my dad not to take me out, but he would not have me involved with the revolution in any way. I am not sure if I would have made it as a player, but my opportunity was truncated by the revolution and its fraudulent and dictatorial actions.

I saw taking Physical Education at Hialeah High as maybe a way to re-energize my dream of becoming a baseball player. My physical education instructor was also the baseball coach and when he saw me play and hit, he asked me if I wanted to join their team. I said yes as fast as I could. He then asked me my age and when I told him I was 18 soon to be 19, he told me that I was not eligible due to my age. That was disappointing because if I could have played, maybe I could have obtained a baseball scholarship to go to college, played in college and maybe been drafted by a professional team. A lot of maybes, but again I was not able to have this opportunity. Later in life I would satisfy some of these anxieties by playing a lot of softball.

Nevertheless, high school was a great experience for me because it gave me the opportunity to improve my English, learn about the American culture and meet a lot of younger classmates. They thought I was cool because I was 19 and they were 15 and 16. The most fun I had was at the chorus class because we went to competitions throughout the state. In one of these competitions in Daytona Beach, I entered the state solo contest and got second place. The judge did not give me the highest marks because he thought I was too theatrical and that distracted him from the quality of my voice. For me that was a compliment and not a negative. I sang two songs in this competition: *Mattinatta*, an Italian canzonetta, and *Júrame*, a Mexican romantic song.

We Cubans wanted to get ahead in the U.S. and not be a burden on the government. At that time the Welfare Department, through the Cuban Refugee Program, was giving every family $100 per month (Today's equivalent of $827) and several pounds of groceries. This was enough to make it for most families, but we only received this help for 3 months because my father and I started to work. I got a part-time job as a bag boy at a grocery store called Grand Union, which was located at SW 8th Street and 5th Avenue in the heart of what it is known today as Little Havana. My pay was $1.00 per hour plus any tips.

I went there after school until around 9:00 PM. After that a friend of my father's got me a job singing at a not-so-good nightclub called Candilejas until 2:00 AM. The next day I was at school at 7:00 AM for my first class of the day American History. All the bag boys at this Grand Union grocery store were young Cubans like me, and the cashiers were young Cuban girls. The managers trained all the bag boys to be cashiers too, and were used as cashiers when the store got busy on Friday nights and Saturdays. The manager was named Mr. Paradise but he was anything but paradise. He knew that we needed those jobs, and he was very abusive and made us work off the clock. Our workday ended at 9:00 PM when the store closed, but he would often want us to clock out at 9:00 PM and then clean the store and make it ready for the next morning. We would get out around 9:30 PM giving the company and Mr. Paradise one half hour of free labor.

One day all of us got together and decided to stop that abuse. Some of us started cleaning at 8:30 PM and some would wait on the customers so that by 9:00 PM we were ready to go home. Mr. Paradise was not happy with this, and he used to inspect the store and find little things wrong in order to keep us longer. It got to a point when we had all the little things taken care of and Mr. Paradise had to let us go at 9:00 PM. Don't mess with Cubans!

The night job was a different story. I sang with a quartette from a very small platform in the corner of this small establishment. The musical group played to an audience, who we never saw because the place was very dark, and all you could hear were "strange" noises, but we could not see anyone. Minors could not work in nightclubs because to do so you needed to have a police card which was only issued to people 21 years or older. Everyone working at night needed this card in the event you were stopped. This, they thought, prevented delinquency. The owner of the establishment, a Cuban of course, was doing me a favor paying me $33 per week for six nights because I was not legally permitted to work there due to my age.

The owner of the nightclub gave me two very simple rules to follow: Do not get in trouble with the customers and told me to keep an eye on him in case the inspectors came in. We arranged a signal for him to alert me of trouble. He would raise his right hand in the air, and when that happened, I was to go out the back door and hide in my car until he would go and get me. I could see him well because the only light in the place was at the cash register where the owner mostly stood. I had to concentrate on my singing and at the same time keep looking at him all the while distracted by those now familiar "strange" noises. It was nerve racking to say the least but we needed the money and I loved to sing.

One night while I was singing a very soft and romantic Cuban Bolero, it happened. His right hand went up in the air. I did not finish the song and ran like a maniac out the backdoor. I hid on the floor of the back seat of our car covered by a blanket. Our car was a 1953 Buick Special, which cost us $100, this money was a gift from our good friend from Boca Ciega, Dr. Jose Abay. There I stayed for over an hour, waiting for the policeman to say: "You in the 1953 white Buick come out with your hands up!"

While in my makeshift hideout, a lot of ideas raced through my mind. The worst thought was the fear of getting deported back to Cuba for breaking the law. I thought of the pain this would bring to my parents who had sacrificed 30 years of their careers to bring me to freedom, all for nothing. But nothing happened. No policeman came to take me away, no owner came to tell me it was all clear. I was scared and confused but finally I mustered enough courage to peek out the back window and I saw nothing. I decided to get out and go back to the nightclub only to learn that it was a false alarm. He was wondering where I had gone. When I told him that he had given me the signal, he apologized and said that he had done it without thinking and there were no inspectors. I thanked the owner for the opportunity and quit. After that I made a solemn promise to never again knowingly break the law no matter the consequences.

On the other hand my father was determined to find a job outside his profession. My uncle Lázaro got both of them jobs as house painters, and they needed to start the next day. Papi (this is what I called him most of the time) was quite excited at the opportunity because he always liked to paint. Not only did he paint beautiful and colorful abstract paintings as a hobby, but he also, on occasions, would paint our house in Boca Ciega Beach as a form of relaxation and exercise.

Papi knew how to paint houses and was determined to make that his new career in the U.S. He went out that night and bought some clothes for the job. The next morning as I was getting ready for school, I heard my uncle laughing like mad. When I went to the living room, Papi was the object of his laughter. Papi came out of his room dressed as an actor dressed in a theatrical role of a painter. He had the typical overalls with suspenders and the typical hat. When asked about his outfit he said; "You always have to dress for the part." Not only was he going to paint for a living, but he was going to look the part. The job only lasted for a few days because Papi was offered a job as Master of Ceremonies and comedian in one of the local Cuban nightclubs. From then until he retired, he worked in his usual acting and entertainment profession where he made a decent living.

Chapter Nine
Visa Waivers or Sweaters

The plane continued its way north toward Chicago. Gradually the earth colors began to change from dark greens to lighter greens, then to light browns, and finally to white. To experience from the air the sight of snow-covered ground was one that my dark Cuban eyes had never experienced before. The large and small frozen lakes I was witnessing were amazing to me, to think of how different the temperature was in Cuba. Havana on average had temperatures in January and February never below 61degrees Fahrenheit and in the summer months, especially in July and August, the maximum temperature hovered around 88 degrees Fahrenheit.

Even to this day every time I see snow or the weather gets a little nippy, I think of my Aunt Lolita, who was an extremely famous and successful actress in Cuba. She left the island months before my family with her husband Lázaro and settled in Miami. In fact it was "Tía Lola" who made all the arrangements for us to leave Cuba. This was typical of most families back then; when one member would leave, this began the quest for getting everyone else in the family out as well. It was hard to openly communicate about the "progress" of the arrangements, because everyone was afraid that the Cuban government was intercepting telephone calls and reading everyone's mail.

Tia Lola, who was very sharp, devised a code to inform us of the arrangements, in other words obtaining our visa waivers. She substituted the word "sweaters" for "visa waivers." She would write letters with sentences like; "I have already started to knit the sweaters you asked me for." She would say on the telephone: "The sweaters should be finished in about 4 months." If some Cuban government officials would read the letters or intercept the phone calls, (which was very doubtful in my opinion), they would probably know that it was a code because one did not obviously need sweaters in Cuba. What we needed were visas. Tia Lola will always have a special place in my heart. She not only provided the "sweaters" but also the plane tickets and many other things after we arrived in Miami, including a fully furnished house in Hialeah for us.

As the plane continued north, I could see more and more snow. Many valleys filled with snow, mountaintops adorned in bright whites and farm fields that seemed to be barren and incapable of producing the next harvest. How could these fields later be reborn and be fruitful again? How could something that looked so dead be brought back to life? There was only one answer, one reason, one force behind it: the hand of God, our Creator, the maker of heaven and earth.

The design of our planet could not be the result of some act of scientific chance. It is the divine design of God. For billions of years and after millions of cataclysms and natural and man-made disasters, our earth, under the watchful eye of its Creator, revives itself, manages to flourish again, and after every cold and desolate winter it comes back again with a warm and sun-filled spring. Looking back at my late adolescence and early youth, I could also see the hand of God working in my life, reviving and renewing me.

Chapter Ten
Cuban refugee, Cuban exile, or Immigrant?

According to the online Dictionary by Farlex (www.thefreedictionary.com) a refugee is defined as "one who flees in search of refuge, as in times of war, political oppression, or religious persecution."

On the other hand according to Wikipedia (en.wikipedia.org/wiki/Exile) Exile "means to be away from one's home, while either being explicitly refused permission to return and/or being threatened with imprisonment or death upon return." An exile can be self-imposed or mandated by the government. Self imposed exile, it also states, is often used as a form of protest.

Amaro and Portes (1972) proposed that "these first refugees (from Cuba) came imagining that exile would be temporary – waiting for the "inevitable" American reaction and help to overthrow Cuba's new government." (Pedraza-Bailey. Page 7) www.latinamericanstudies.org/exile/portrait.pdf)

In others words, we (Cubans) came as refugees, and after many years of countless disappointments have become exiles. We were not immigrants because an immigrant comes to better him or herself in the new country. Cubans in the first few years of the communist revolution came to impoverish themselves both economically, socially, and family wise. Thoughts of going back after democracy was re-established remained the force that made us endure the rigors of a self-imposed exile. I strongly believe that most of the Cubans who came as refugees to the U.S. did not want to stay in the U.S. permanently.

Therefore, Cubans who came first were not immigrants and cannot be compared to any other immigration to the U.S. They do not even compare to those Cubans that came after 1980. Many of these later arrivals did not have a political opposition to the communist government, but economical and social reasons for leaving the island. They saw coming to the U.S. as an opportunity to get out of the economic fiasco found in Cuba today. The proof can be seen in the sheer number of them who went back to visit Cuba as soon as the law allowed them to do so. They also, still to this day, collectively send large amounts of money to their relatives in Cuba. All of these actions define them more as immigrants rather than exiles.

Back when my family and I arrived in the early 60s the U.S. treated us as refugees, because we were just that. However, the U.S. continues to treat those that are coming now the same way even though they are now immigrants. These immigrants are treated differently than those from other countries, because they get the benefits of the law of "Ajuste Cubano" (Cuban Adjustment). Many of the new arrivals enter the U.S. illegally by the Mexican or Canadian borders, and once they are here, they are processed very quickly and quite legally.

Coming to the U.S. as a political refugee in 1962 was quite different than it was during the latter part of the twentieth century and the beginning of the twenty first century. The attitude toward the U.S. was and is quite different. In 1962 we were grateful to the U.S. for helping us out of the hell that Cuba had become. Latecomers, for the most part, come demanding help and entitlements and do not show too much gratitude for the hospitality. In my humble opinion, this law should be changed. Let the Cuban immigrants be treated as any other immigrant.

Chapter Eleven
My Second Visit to California

As I was heading toward the end of this flight, the plane was approaching San Diego International Airport's only runway by San Diego Bay. I saw the Pacific Ocean for the second time in my life. San Diego Bay was filled with many U.S. Navy ships. This view made me think of two important episodes in my life: My first visit to California and my experience in the military.

It was around May 1963 and I had finished my one school year at Hialeah Senior High School. I was an average student. All I needed to graduate was to go to night school in the fall and take English Composition. Around that same time, due to an economic slowdown in South Florida, I had lost my job. My Aunt Lolita and Uncle Lázaro had also lost their jobs and things were getting quite tense at home. We were now living together with my Aunt Lolita and her family at her house in West Hialeah. I had to sleep on the sofa in the living room because there were 10 of us living in the same house. I had no money, no future, and the home situation was not helping my self-esteem. I was getting really depressed.

One afternoon after spending the day looking for a job, I stopped at a Cuban cafeteria around Calle Ocho to drink a shot of Cuban coffee. There I ran into my good friend from Boca Ciega, Alvaro Quiroga. We exchanged greetings and also told each other about how bad things were. Alvaro told me that the following week he was going to Los Angeles, California where he had contacted two of our other neighborhood friends, Felo Dalmau and Bachun Hidalgo. They were now living in LA. They told him he could stay with them until he found a job. My good friend also told me that he was looking for somebody to go with him to help him drive and also share the cost of the trip. Without any hesitation I told him he had just found that person and volunteered for the "job." He accepted with the condition that the two friends in LA approve it. Alvaro later called them and Felo and Bachun gave us the okay. California here I come!

The question now was how do I tell my parents that I was going. I had never been apart from them and I knew this news was going to be hard for them to take. I went home and told them. At first they were very negative, especially my mother. As we discussed the alternatives further, both agreed and started helping me to prepare for the trip. The first obstacle was of course, money. I needed money to pay for half the gas, lodging, food and other necessities.

The average price of gas in 1963 was around $0.30 per gallon. So for a trip of almost 3,000 miles, driving a very small four-cylinder Anglia English Ford, (assuming 30 miles per gallon usage) we needed around 100 gallons or $15.00 each. We estimated that the trip was going to take around five days with four nights of lodging, so we needed around $5.00 per night each or $20.00 for lodging. Finally food for 5 days I estimated at $7.00 per day each or $35.00. This would give us an approximate total of $70.00 each. All I could acquire was $50.00 that my mother gave me. She also made me some food for the trip.

We left Miami and 58 hours later we were entering LA. We had to cut a lot of corners on the trip, such as sleeping in the car, skipping meals and looking for the cheapest motels and food joints. We did some crazy things on the trip. We crossed the Arizona desert in the middle of the day, and we encountered a sand storm in El Indio, New Mexico. The worst part was that we were forced to drive the car after the sand storm not being able to see well through the damaged windshield caused by the sand, but we made it. I made it to LA with $20.00 to my name, no high school diploma, but with three great friends and the strength and free spirit that only young men have.

Chapter Twelve
Los Angeles was hard for me

My plans to marry my fiancée, Angela, and bring her over to the U.S. had to be postponed until I was financially secure. California was a fresh start for me. My first priority was to get a job that could support me and then try to fulfill my childhood dream: making it big in Hollywood as a movie star. I felt I was in the right place given that Hollywood is part of what they call Greater LA. The first part of my plan worked well, and Alvaro and I got a job at the same plastic factory (Olympic Plastics) where our other two friends worked. We later moved into a larger apartment in Culver City across the Metro Goldwin Mayer Studios.

Because we were spending a lot of money eating out, I came up with the idea to cook our own meals to save money. The problem was that none of us knew how to cook, so I said, "How hard can it be to cook?" Then we divided the house chores. I would do the groceries and cook, and the others would do the dishes, clean the apartment, and take the clothes to the Laundromat. I called my mother and got some of her Cuban cuisine recipes and I was up and running. In short I became a very respectable Cuban cook. It was actually fun. These skills would come very handy later in life.

I worked at this factory during the third shift. It started at 11:30 PM and ended at 7:30 AM. In the department called Injection, we made all kinds of plastic parts and models. The foreman was a white American man, and the mold installer was a black American man from the section called Watts. The operators were all young black American women also from Watts. My job was to assist everyone in the department and do whatever I was told to do. Because their English pronunciation was a lot different than what I had learned in school, I had a lot of trouble understanding my co-workers.

Many times they would tell me something and I did not get a word of it. The women laughed at me and called me a crazy Cuban. I laughed back and as time went by, I started to understand them better and we had a good time. It was hard work, and I had no chance for promotion unless I wanted to inherit the mold installer's job. One day the foreman asked me if I knew how to drive a forklift. I said yes, of course, even though I had no idea how to do it, but when you need a job, you never say no. I had seen others drive it, and I had a pretty good idea, but I was not aware that the steering wheel worked backwards. I lifted a tall stack of finished product, and I was told to drive it to the warehouse. Lifting it was a piece of cake. Driving forward was also easy. Turning the corner was a catastrophe because I turned the wheel to the right, but the forklift turned left onto a stack of materials instead. The steering wheel did not turn the front wheels, but the rear ones. My entire load fell to the floor.

During my breaks and lunch I would read the newspaper section where they announced casting calls. Most of them were early in the morning, so I would finish work at 7:30 AM, drive home to change, and then go to the casting call, but I was always too late. People were standing in line since the night before. Many times I waited in the long lines on the street for many hours to no avail. When I was getting close to the entrance door, someone would inevitably come out and thank us for our interest. They had found what they needed. I did this for at least 50 times until I grew tired of it and I gave up on my dream. Looking back, I should have tried harder, but I did not. Such is life.

While there I also made contact with a high school classmate, Alex Carasa, who lived with his family in nearby Santa Barbara. This city is about 95 miles and one and one half hours north of LA. Most Saturday mornings when I finished at the factory, I would borrow a car and drive to Santa Barbara for the weekend. The Carasa family was great! They treated me as family. Sunday night I would typically drive back to LA to return the borrowed car before the start of the workday on Monday. I have many fond memories of these weekend trips.

Chapter Thirteen
Mixed Results in Santa Barbara, California

After three months working at Olympic Plastics, I was given a layoff notice. My foreman told me that they did that every year and that in a few weeks they would call everyone back to work. I could not wait a few weeks without pay because we had expenses to pay at the apartment, and I did not have any savings on reserve. I was again back where I started. I called my friend Alex in Santa Barbara to tell him about the latest news, and when I did his mother got on the phone and asked me to go and live with them until I found another job. The offer was tempting because I really liked Santa Barbara and this family was very warm and reminded me of mine. I took the offer and rode a bus to Santa Barbara.

I got there and they had fixed a bed in one of the rooms for me. Mrs. Carasa had fixed a well-prepared typical Cuban meal, which I had not had for a long time. The next day I bought the newspaper and started to look for a job. I found one, which read: "Assistant gardener needed for a private home $75 per week." The average hourly rate in 1963 was around $2.25 per hour, so this was below the average hourly rate, but above the minimum wage of $1.25, at approximately $1.90 per hour, but I was attracted to it because it seemed like something I could do and would not be so hard. On occasions

I had worked in our garden and yard in our home in Cuba, and I liked being outdoors. Also I thought, how hard would I have to work as assistant gardener? I thought that after cutting the grass and cultivating the flowers, I would have time to relax by the pool drinking an iced tea.

I went for the interview and I was hired. I went back to the Carasa's with the good news, and Mr. Carasa laughed at me when I said the part about the pool and the iced tea. He told me, given his many years working, that I was in for a surprise. The home where I was hired had four acres of land mostly covered by oak trees. It had very limited grassy areas and about 10 different flowerbeds. My first impression was that I was right, and Mr. Carasa was wrong.

This was an easy job I thought when I met the gardener in charge, a Mexican-American named Don Manuel. He spoke very little English, and he was about 50 years old, but in very good shape. The first day of work was great. All I did was water the flowerbeds, cleaned them and pruned the dry leaves and branches. I got home that afternoon and when I told them about my day, all of them were happy for me, except Mr. Carasa, who was still skeptical and insisted that I would be surprised very soon.

Mr. Lorenzo Carasa was like a prophet. The next day I was told by Don Manuel what the real reason for my hiring was. He explained that the owner wanted to relocate the septic tank from the top of one of the hills near the house to the bottom of that same hill which was about 100 feet away. Don Manuel proceeded to plan how we (meaning I) were going to do it.

We would put a stake at the edge of the existing septic tank and one near the new location. We would then run a rope tied to both stakes which would mark where I needed to dig a

2 feet wide by 3 feet deep trench for 100 feet down the hill in the month of August when the average temperature in the hills near Santa Barbara was around 100 degrees Fahrenheit. This project was a far cry from sitting by the pool drinking iced tea. After work I decided to again enroll to finish high school. I did it at Santa Barbara Senior High School in their night program. Without this diploma I was not going to ever get a good-paying job.

It took me about one month to finish the project because we found a lot of rocks in the path, and it was very hard to dig into them. We had to make the trench going around some of the bigger rocks and with many curves and not a straight line as planned. I did not quit because I was still convinced that the pool and the iced tea were coming after I finished this hard job. After the trench was finished, Don Manuel and I laid down the plastic pipe. It was hard due to all the different angles and turns of the trench, but we finished it and it was inspected by the city. To my surprise, it passed the inspection. We then covered the trench and the pipe and planted new grass. A plumber came later and made the hook up. The project was a success and the owner came to congratulate Don Manuel and me and gave us a $50.00 bonus each.

The next day I came in and I was ready for the pool and the iced tea, but instead Don Manuel gave me a ladder, a safety harness and line, and a large heavy duty brush and told me that the next project was to clean all the oak trees of a fungus that they had contracted. I looked at Don Manuel with a smile, thanked him for his help and quit. Again I was back where I started.

In no time I found another job due to my "vast experience as a gardener" as a foreman of a group of gardeners for a lawn maintenance company that serviced private homes. I was also paid $75.00 per week. I had to drive a pickup truck full of lawn service equipment. On it I would transport my crew composed of mostly illegal immigrants to the different homes and after getting instructions from the owners of the homes, I would try to explain to each of the members of my crew, in Spanish, what to do. The problem was that my Spanish was different that their Spanish, and their level of comprehension was very low even in Spanish. For the most part they were good people and hard working individuals trying to survive like me. I would assign the last home for me to do, so I was a working foreman. Titles are sometimes deceiving!

Since I now had a better job, I bought a used car with the help of some friends. It was a 1956 cream colored Ford Fairlane two-door hard top. I had borrowed the money to buy it from these friends and I was paying them back weekly. I also had another job. I was an instructor of Cuban dances. Some of Carasa's friends were Mexican-American and Central American young girls who wanted to learn how to dance Cuban rhythms. I would have a class of about 10 of them once a week, and they would try to learn Mambo, Cha-Cha-Cha, Bolero, Rumba and Conga. Some of my training was paying off!

One day an American girl came to the class, and she was a ballet and modern dance student, but wanted to also learn Cuban dance. She learned very fast and she was a great dancer. She asked me if I wanted to be her partner at a show that was going to be part of a festival called La Fiesta which happened in Santa Barbara every year. That sounded great, so we got a hold of a record with a great arrangement of Agustin Lara's Granada, and between the two of us choreographed a modern dance routine with a Spanish flavor. Our performance was very well accepted and we even got a write up in the local paper. In the paper article they mentioned my entertainment background in Cuba, which was very gratifying.

From that write up Mr. Remigio Velazquez, who had a two-hour radio show every Sunday afternoon, contacted me. Mr. Velazquez wanted me to sing and recite poetry, etc on the show, but told me that he could not pay me for now. I agreed to do it hoping that it would lead to bigger and better things. It was fun to do it and I did it for a while. I was not progressing financially even though the Carasas' did not want to charge me anything for living with them. At least once per week I would go and buy some groceries, which made me feel better. My salary was too small and my plans to marry Angela and bring her to the U.S. were still a far away dream.

Chapter Fourteen
Homesick for Miami.
Back to Miami

During my stint in California I would often talk to my parents on the phone. On one particular day while speaking with my father he mentioned something to me that made me think. He said to me: "Things are better in South Florida now; you are working as a gardener in California, but you could also work as a gardener here, near your mother and me. We can be together again. Think about it and come back home." I thought about it long and hard and decided to return to South Florida.

I called my parents back to tell them about my decision, but the only problem was I did not have the money for the bus fare. They sent me the money, I sold (gave) my car back to the friend who had lent me the money and I came back to sunny Florida in a 58 hour Greyhound bus ride. That was a trip I would never recommend not even to my worst enemy. This trip was made even harder because I was coming back feeling a lot like a failure. I had to drop out of high school for the third time and I was back where I started again.

The conference in San Diego, which was for a week, was great. Its content was very helpful to me. The knowledge I acquired was going to help me improve many procedures back at my job. I met very interesting people at the conference and many of them asked me about Miami. They were curious about me and the city I was from. I told them that Miami was like any other city. It had its good and bad points. I also told them not to believe everything they read or heard from the media. Some of them were more interested in my heritage and asked me questions about Cuba.

Back in my hotel room that night, I started to remember all the things that I had experienced in Miami. I had left it in 1963 and had traveled to California for better economic opportunities.

Coming back to Miami in early 1964 finding it economically stronger was very encouraging. When I came back from California, Miami had changed. The Cuban community was now stronger and there were many jobs available. I found a job at a large grocery store called A & P. It was a full-time position in the produce department as a clerk. The produce department handled all the fresh vegetables and fruits. I had to start at 6:00 AM and have the displays ready by 9:00 AM by the time the store opened. The store was located at SW 8th street and 22nd Avenue in Miami.

A friend who had worked with me at Grand Union, referred me to the union steward she knew from A & P where she now worked, and this man got me the job. A & P was an open shop where employees had the choice of joining the union or not. First I did not because I could not afford the fees. I needed every bit of my check and did not want anything taken out. I was in my 30-day probation period. Besides, I was also doing quite well and the manager had given me a great review and a small raise. A & P was a big company back then and the manager told me that he would help me move up the ranks as I continued to learn more about the grocery business.

One day the union steward visited me. He pressured me into joining the union by reminding me that he was the one who had gotten me the job. That is when I joined. Several weeks later my manager told me that my hours would be cut and that I had been transferred to the store located at SW 40 Street and 122nd Avenue several miles away and farther from my home. This was obviously in retaliation for joining the union. I called the steward to complain and he told me that there was nothing he could do. I told him to take me out of the union, given that he could not help me and I did not see any benefits by me staying in it. Several weeks later my original position was given back to me and I was happy again. I did not know this then, but my boss' action was a totally illegal practice.

I enrolled in Hialeah High School's night program to try to finish and get my diploma. My life was getting somewhat better and my plans of a wedding were now closer than ever. My parents were also working and doing much better so were my aunt and uncle.

I bought a little used car at Biltmore Motors where the owner, our good friend, Ramon Rodriguez, gave us a great deal. He is still a long-time friend.

Things were going better for me at work and they were about to get better. A classmate from the year I spent in Hialeah High, Miguel Pino, called me one day and knowing that I could sing, asked me if I wanted to join the band where he was playing. I told him yes because I always had that urge to perform. There has always been something inside of me that pushes me in that direction. I went to one of their rehearsals at the house of Arnoldo Velazquez in West Hialeah. They asked me to sing a couple of songs and I was accepted by its leader Frank (Panchín) Saenz. The band was composed at the time of 8 members: Panchín playing the electric guitar and sax, José (Pepe) Pino playing the bass guitar, Miguel Pino, Arnold Velazquez, Willie Trueba, and Luis (Wichy) Puga in percussion. Manuel (Manolito) Lopez-Font and Omar Blanco, were the two trumpets. The new member, me made it a group of 9. It was called: Conjunto Tropical.

Chapter Fifteen
Añorada Cuba and other very important events

The conference was finished, and I was on my way back to the airport in San Diego for my trip back home. These last few days had gone by really fast, but not as fast as the days and months after I got back to Miami from California. In the first half of 1964 I experienced very important events in my life. These months had gone by so quickly that now, while I was remembering them, I had a hard time remembering their sequence. I experienced life-changing events that were to shape and diagram the rest of my life. Getting on the plane and sitting down for a long trip back gave me some additional time to meditate and reminisce with a very profound and intense desire to remember as much as possible.

Playing with "Conjunto Tropical" became quite enjoyable. We played many parties and dances. We had a unique mixture of music because we could not only play traditional Cuban music, but also the American music hits of the time. Not many bands could do the same, so we were in demand and normally played as the "second" band in many of the Cuban community dances.

We continued to rehearse at Arnoldo Velazquez's home. His parents and family had given us all the accommodations to do so in their carport. Many of the neighbors would also come and listen to us play. Arnoldo, who died a short time ago and is now with the Lord, became one of my best friends.

I decided to continue my guitar studies with Professor Leopoldo Ramos and one day he invited me to a get together at the home of a composer named Cristina Saladrigas. At this jam session there were several guitar players and singers interpreting their music and songs. Cristina introduced her song called: "Añorada Cuba" to the group and it was a big hit. I fell in love with it and asked Professor Ramos in my next class to help me learn it. I thought it would be a big hit for our band given our audience and the timely lyrics. I brought the song to our next rehearsal and everyone liked it a lot. Panchin, our leader made some changes to the harmony and introduction and made it even better.

During those days at the Immaculate Conception Catholic Church in Hialeah there was a Cuban priest by the name of Padre Jorge B. Chabebe who was organizing a group of parishioners to come up with ideas to help young Cubans. They had been very disoriented and confused due to all the changes in their lives. He met with several of the volunteers and formed what was called: "Las Instituciones Católicas de la Parroquia de La Inmaculada Concepción." (Immaculate Conception Parrish's Catholic Institutions).

Padre Chabebe would talk to everybody and ask for ideas and help from anyone he would meet. He wanted to do projects to help the Cuban youth seek solace in the Church and also help them maintain the traditions, language, and culture of Cuba. One of the members of the institutions was Maria Dolores (Beba) Pernas, a devout Catholic and a person dedicated to the youth. One night Beba was visiting with Raul Ballester, a well-known choreographer and dancer who she had met while he was designing the choreography for a

"Comparsa" (Group Dance) in Cuba. Raul lived very close to the Velazquez's home and while they were talking, they heard us playing. They came over and were there for a while. Beba put two-and-two together and asked Raul if he would help her form a "Comparsa" using our band. The idea was taken to Padre Chabebe and he liked it. They spoke to us and we agreed to help. When they heard the song "Añorada Cuba" they proposed to Father Chabebe that he should use that title song and name the show "Añorada Cuba" with the blessings of the composer.

At the same time Padre Chabebe was talking and soliciting help from Pili de la Rosa and Demetrio Menendez, both involved working with dubbing English speaking TV programs in Spanish for a company that was producing these in Miami. Pili de la Rosa came up with the idea of having the youth lip sync the famous songs of Cuba throughout its history.

Both ideas were blended into one show and the word was put out that they were starting rehearsals for this show. At first just a few young people showed up, but after a while the word was out and they had many wanting to participate. The rehearsals took many months.

Things were looking up for me. I had a good job, I had finally finished high school at night, I was playing almost every weekend with the band, and I was involved with a show. Given all that, I decided to ask Angela to come to the U.S. and marry me at last. I felt I was now ready and able. I called her and told her expecting that she would be very happy, but that was not the case. To my surprise she told me that she was not coming because she could not leave her mother alone in Cuba. At first I tried to convince her, but after a while I got the message and realized that she no longer loved me after having been away from each other such a long time. This was very hard to take, but I stopped insisting. This event set me back emotionally during a time when things were working pretty well.

My involvement with "Añorada Cuba" was giving me a lot of pleasure and helped me cope with the aftermath of the breakup with Angela. My life felt empty at the time and doing something to help others seemed to help fill some of the gaps. One of the initial rules for the show was that no one would get any compensation for their work. Everyone was a volunteer. We were there to help those in need.

Eventually Beba Pernas took the members of the band under her wing and we would frequent her home regularly to plan and sometimes just to talk. Beba was a very knowledgeable person with a degree in psychology and a deep biblical and religious knowledge. She began to evangelize us without us knowing it. She would patiently listen to all of us and she was like an older sister helping us cope with all the anxieties of the time.

Both Beba and her husband Alfredo had gone to something called "Cursillos of Christianity." This was a 4-day program similar to a retreat where the participants would experience talks given by lay and religious speakers. More importantly, it was an instrument of conversion. Cursillos was started in the island of Mallorca, in Spain by a layman by the name of Eduardo Bonnin (Same last name as my maternal grandmother, Coloma, who was also born in Mallorca) and the movement spread through most of the world and it had started a Spanish-speaking program in the Diocese of Miami.

In June of 1964 I did not qualify to go to Cursillos given that the minimum age was 21. Beba invited me to go to Cursillos and called the leadership of the movement to get a waiver. I had not been a practicing Catholic most of my life. I was baptized, did my first communion and the confirmation, but there it pretty much stopped. Our family was Catholic in name only, and we were not regularly involved with the Church. We would go to Church maybe twice per year or for weddings, baptisms, funerals, or the like. We were what is called: "Catolicos a nuestra manera" (Catholics in our own way). There was some hesitation on the part of the leadership because of that, but Beba insisted and told them that I was a good candidate and that I had the leadership capabilities. She convinced them my going through the experience would be a positive influence on the rest of our group and my own family.

Beba prevailed and I was invited to participate in the Cursillo number 15 of men. The weekend coincided with The Fourth of July weekend, which was a Saturday. I asked for Friday off at work and my father drove me to the parking lot of Saint Michael's Church in Miami where all of us participants took a bus that took us to an old World War II barrack (#60) at the Opalocka Airport. This location was used because it had two floors. The conference room, the dining room and the kitchen were on the first floor and the beds were on the second floor. Each floor had a bathroom. The barrack was not in very good condition given that it was first used in the 1940s, but it served the purpose for Cursillos. We had to stay there until Sunday night without leaving the place.

Cursillo #15 was a life-changing event for me and for most of those who participated in this very intense method of evangelization and leadership training. As the days passed and we were absorbing all the "rollos" (talks), the intensity grew and that heterogeneous group of men, both the participants and the team that was serving us, became closer and closer together. The Grace of the Holy Spirit was working in our souls and little by little this group of men accepted Christ as their savior, and were converted. My moment came right after Father Miguel de Arrillaga's "rollo" about The Seven Sacraments, which lasted four hours. Padre Miguel was great and his way of presenting this difficult subject opened my mind and my heart. I surrendered my heart to Christ. I went to confession after many years of ignoring God. Padre Miguel was also a very influential person to me in years to come. These three days changed my life in more ways than I could possibly realize back then.

I got out of Cursillo with fire in my heart, love in my soul, and a strong desire that others around me experience what I had experienced. The moment I got home I started inviting my parents and all my family. At the next rehearsal, I invited all the members of the band. People had a hard time accepting my change. I was obviously different. I guess they wanted to see if I was for real, or if it was just a fleeting high I was on. They wondered if my newfound zeal for God would fizzle away. At first they would not accept my invitation to go to Cursillo, but as time went by and they saw that I was persevering, one by one started to fall in the net. First there was my father, then my mother and a few other members of the family. The band members went all together and participated in Cursillo #21. Christ had used Beba Pernas to help me find Him and I was the imperfect instrument to bring others to the flock. All of them brought others and our family and friends were growing strong in the faith. My father was also moved by the fire of the Spirit and became a very strong force of Christian renewal and commitment inside the entertainment field

Añorada Cuba in the meantime had its debut in August 1964 at the Milander Auditorium in Hialeah. It was a tremendous success and people stood in line to get tickets that were sold for just $0.50. At that price everyone could afford to see us. Given the success, we needed a larger venue, so Padre Chabebe and his leadership group took a big leap of faith and decided to present the show at the largest venue in Miami at the time, the Dade County Auditorium. This auditorium seated around 2,500 people and was very expensive to rent, but they did it and in September 1964 we performed there to a full house for many shows. The tickets were now $1.00 and stayed at that price for many performances.

Añorada Cuba was the vehicle that got me to Cursillo and Cursillo was responsible for me finding, my life-long love and companion. How that happened was proof that there is no such thing as coincidence. God's plan sometimes uses methods that at first seem backwards, but in the end workout. When my mother went to her Cursillo, impacted her greatly. She was so full of the Holy Spirit and she was very happy to see me and my father on a different path than before. The night she got out of her Cursillo she could not stop talking about her experiences. She told me that she had met this young woman at Cursillo who really impressed her. She was one of the presenters even though she was very young. She said to me; "I have to introduce you to her." Not only because she was greatly impressed by this young woman, but also because she looked a lot like my ex-fiancé Angela.

Mothers are always trying to fix their children up with somebody they know, so I said to her; "Come on Mom, I do not need that now." Besides, I thought, she probably did not look anything like Angela, but even if she did, that was the last thing I needed. I was slowly getting Angela out of my mind, and my life, and I did not need my mother's good intentions to slow down the progress I had made. One night that we were going to an "Ultreya" (Meeting of many groups), she saw this young lady and stopped her, so she could meet me. She said: "Yolandita let me introduce to you my son Rolando. Roly, this is the young lady I told you about; "doesn't she look like Angela?" I was ready to die of embarrassment, but I managed to say hello and be polite.

After that awkward episode, I told my mother that this Yolandita did not look anything like Angela. She was very attractive, though she seemed sort of shy by the way she was dressed and how she acted. To this day I believe that my mother felt something special with Yolandita that had nothing to do with what she looked like, but a lot to do with what would happen later. I continued to run into Yolandita at many of the events because she was part of the leadership (Secretariado) of Cursillos. She was the youngest member of the leadership and she acted much older than her age.

I later found out from my mother-in-law, Tete, that I had met Yolandita before. When both my mother and Tete were pregnant with me and Yolandita, they met in Cojimar. It turned out that Tete was a friend of a neighbor of my aunt Rina and while Tete was visiting her friend we were also visiting Rina. Tete asked her friend to introduce her to my mother and father and the two mothers shook hands and exchanged small talk. My mother commented that she wanted a girl and Tete said she wanted a boy. Neither got their wish. Was this meeting a coincidence? Did my mother's instincts react to Yolandita due to this meeting? Who knows?

At that time I was going steady with one of the members of Añorada Cuba. She was one of the dancers, a very pretty and smart young lady. Her name will remain unsaid for obvious reasons. We had a very good relationship, and she was a really sweet and warm person. She was also a fantastic dancer and I really enjoyed dancing with her at all the parties we went to as a couple. I invited her to Cursillos, but for some reason she did not want to go. Her parents had a very strong influence on her, maybe more than normal, and they did not approve of Cursillos. I insisted many times but to no avail. Changing the tactics I called my "friend" Yolandita to ask her for a favor. I said: "Can you call my girlfriend and invite her to Cursillo; maybe coming from you, a stranger, she would go." Yolandita called, but she never went. She later broke up with me due to another unrelated issue.

One day my father and I went to a picnic sponsored by Cursillo and somehow my father and I started to talk with Yolandita for a long time. After that conversation and on the way home, my father remarked how pretty she was and how smart and committed to Christ she was. I agreed with him and started to think about her a lot. I was concerned because I did not know how old she was. If she was older than me, I had very little chance that she would accept going out with me. In any event, I was very interested in her.

My father, my mother, and I were invited to participate in the Cursillo's school for presenters (Escuela de Profesores). This was a course given every Wednesday night, at Gesu Church downtown Miami. This meeting was to prepare us to be part of the team that would go to a Cursillo and help the participants in different ways. At this school I got to see Yolanda, as I called her in my mind, and many times I found ways to talk to her and at times volunteer for some work that I knew she would be also doing. By the way she looked at me, I knew that she was attracted to me as I was to her, but I kept silent respecting her leadership position, and I also was not yet sure how old she was. One day I noticed she had, what looked like a wedding band on her left ring finger and my heart stopped. She was married, I said. I knew it. This was too good to be true.

My newfound spirituality prevented me to desire someone else's wife, so I went to confession many times trying to obtain strength and overcome this attraction. One day I went with a group that was going to visit a nun's convent in Central Florida where some of our sisters in Cursillo had gone to become nuns. I volunteered to be one of the drivers of the bus that was taking the group on this pilgrimage. After my turn to drive ended, I sat by Yolanda for a long time and we talked a lot. I found out that she was not married and that she was my age, but I also found out that the reason she was wearing a ring, was because she had made known some very preliminary intentions to become a nun also. I do not know if I felt better or worse at the news.

Now I understood why she was reserved and shy. Now I could see why she was so devoted and why she was in a leadership position at her young age. My spiritual director at the time told me that there was nothing wrong with what I felt for her because she was not a nun yet. This news gave me some hope. Inside of me I felt that she also had feelings for me, so I decided to let her know how I felt and told her that I thought about her all the time and that every time our eyes met, I felt a tingling sensation in my heart. She was visibly upset and got really red. She told me that it was not possible because she was going a different route in her Christian vocation. Somehow what she was saying did not match the look in her eyes. Those beautiful eyes were saying that she also had feelings for me, but she was afraid due to two things: my very unstable love history and the fact that I was a new convert who might not persevere in the faith for long.

Those were two very legitimate concerns and I asked her if she had them. She denied it, but I did not believe her. She told me that it was due to her vocation and had nothing to do with me. Something was telling me that she was the one. My mother had felt it when they met. She also impressed my father. I found her to be extremely attractive, smart, warm, spiritual, and family oriented. I was ready to do what I could to prove to her that I had changed and I was serious about her.

At that time Yolanda's spiritual director was none other than Padre Miguel, who was also the general spiritual director for Cursillo. Knowing this, I asked Padre Miguel for an appointment to go to confession with him. He gave me the appointment and when I told him about my feelings for Yolanda, he got really upset and told me that I had no right to come between God and Yolanda. I responded that if Yolanda was to be for God, who was I to be the cause of a change in her plans? He then pretty much "ordered me" to stay away from her. Two things came out of this meeting: The first was that Padre Miguel was only thinking of Yolanda's vocations and not about my side of the issue. The second was that his reaction could only be explained if Yolanda had gone to him and expressed doubts about her plans given my presence in her life. Both of these reasons gave me even more vigor and desire to continue to try to convince her.

One Sunday (June 20, 1965) I was giving Yolanda a ride to her home after Mass and when we got to her home I told her in the car that I loved her and that I wanted her to be the mother of my children. She was visibly shaken by my words and I could see a tear on her eyes. We looked at each other intensely and after a brief staring contest, I kissed her so very gently. She said: "No, please no. Stop!" and I said: "No, I will not. I love you and you love me. " Then she finally said yes.

We talked for a long time before I accompanied her to her door on the second floor of the apartment building where she lived with her Mom, Tete and her cousin Terina. She asked me not to say anything because she wanted to keep our love a secret. I protested, but she insisted and asked me to give her some time to absorb this change. I reluctantly agreed.

Several weeks went by and the situation had not changed. Yolanda was afraid of what others would think of her. She was afraid because some of her friends (they were supposed to be my friends too) had told her not to become my girlfriend and told her all kinds of bad things I had done in the past before the Cursillo. On the other hand I was sure that she was the one for me. One night we were going to a going-away party for a priest and Terina, her cousin, was going with us. Attending that party were all our friends from Cursillo; Padre Miguel was also there, and all the leadership team that was mostly against our relationship. I used this opportunity to once and for all, publicly announce that we loved each other. I told her what I was planning to do that day and she begged me not to do it, so when we entered the hall, I grabbed her hand and we walked in hand-in-hand. She tried to slip her hand out of my grasp, but I pressed on until everyone saw us. Most everyone there came to congratulate us and Yolanda felt a big relief. I felt great that now I could scream to the four winds that we were in love.

Around those days I also found a new job. My soon to be brother in law, Vicente (Pupy) Calle had a car wholesale business with his father and brother. Pupy referred me to the used car sales manager of Deel Ford in Coral Gables named Jim Jordan for a job as a salesman. This was a job new to me, but they needed someone who spoke Spanish in order to service the growing Cuban community in South Florida. I got the job and I started to be train by probably the "best actors" I had ever known, in the "art" of selling used cars. Most of the sales force was much older than me and had a lot of experience in how to sell. The job paid well, if you sold, because it was strictly on a commission basis. We got a $75.00 per week draw against future commissions in the event we did not sell anything that week.

I contacted a lot of my friends and my father's friends and I was doing really well. I was selling around 6 cars per month and averaging around $2,000 per month. They also gave me one of the cars from the lot to drive home and for the weekends. During those days Yolanda and I got engaged, and we were making plans for a December 1965 wedding. I was doing pretty well financially, and even though I could not outsell any of the others, I was happy with the money and not too happy with the work. I had to have my eyes open all the time to try to prevent my fellow salesmen from stealing my customers. It was a rough business! It was even rougher because of my Christian beliefs that did not allow me to lie.

In the meantime Añorada Cuba was continuing to be a success and we were invited to visit several cities outside of Miami. We traveled to Gainesville, Florida and performed at the University of Florida. We were invited to perform at the newly opened Lincoln Center in New York City and several other places. Due to this success, many of the people in the leadership of Añorada Cuba, including Padre Chabebe, started what I consider a change in the original plan for the show: to bring the youth closer to God, help them preserve their cultural values. They wanted to change to a more "show business" plan. Success in the performing field many times leads to changes in values and attitudes, and this group was no different. "If it ain't broke, don't fix it."

Someone came up with the idea to change the show and create a new format with new music, new songs, new dances, etc. The old saying "If it is not broken, do not fix it" was ignored. We were playing at full houses everywhere we went. Our fans were not tired of the format, but somehow the leadership decided to change it. In my humble opinion, this was the beginning of the end of Añorada Cuba as it was first conceived. We started to practice the new numbers. Our band was, as in the first show, part of the second half or what we called the "live" part.

One of the premises of the show was that it would be patriotic, but not political. We were not to support or endorse any of the different political factions operating in Miami, nor were we to mention any of the problems associated with Cuba's past and present political history. It was just a musical and cultural show with a religious bend to it. This way we would get the support of all Cubans and we would help all Cubans find their way back to God and keep their heritage. I am not going to go into all the details as to what happened because it is not necessary in my opinion, but the first part of the new show violated these principles and was presenting in their first act a distorted history lesson favoring one of these political groups.

When I saw that part in the dress rehearsal the day before the debut of the new show, I was not only surprised, but really upset. I went to Padre Chabebe and told him to find someone else to sing the title song because I was resigning effective immediately unless that part was changed. I asked him to modify the show and portray the real history or remove me altogether from the show. Padre Chabebe told me that it could not be changed just the day before the debut, and asked me not to quit. In respect to him, I did the show, but it was to be

98

my last one. No one is indispensable, and the show continued without me and some of my friends from the band who had also quit. In my opinion Añorada Cuba, would still be functioning today if they would have not changed its purpose and focus.

Chapter Sixteen
"Greetings from the U.S. Army"
How did my military experience
start/who pushed me?

When I arrived at San Diego's airport on my second trip to California (Chapter 11), and I saw all the Navy ships in the harbor, I remembered the two years I had spent in the U.S. Army. Those two years were very important to me and shaped my character and greatly influenced the way I was to live the rest of my life. The unusual and unexpected way I entered the service was indicative of how important those formative two years would prepare me for what was to come in my future.

During the first months of our engagement, Yolanda, who was working as a secretary for the Cuban Refugee Program at the Welfare Department in Miami, asked me if I was registered for the Selective Service. This was a routine question she asked of any male who was being aided in her office. She explained that it was an obligation for every male over 18 years of age to register. The war in Viet Nam was going on and the draft was in place. My answer was very simple, no. It was my unfounded conviction that the rule did not apply to me because I was just a political refugee with a temporary waiver visa and not a permanent resident of the U.S..

Yolanda assured me that I was wrong. Maybe the first of many times that she would be right and I would be wrong.

She further explained that even though my assumption was logical, logic had nothing to do with some of the rules of the U.S. government. The law included every male including Cuban refugees. In other words, I was breaking the law by not registering at the age of 18 when I first arrived. I was now 21 and not wanting to be outside of the law, so I went and registered for the draft. When I was at the Selective Service office I asked the clerk if I was going to be penalized for the delay, but all she said that as a result I might be called faster than others.

In less than a month I received the notification to take the required physical examination. I began to get worried and a little scared about where all this was going. What would have happened if I had not registered? I would never know. Even though I was in very good health, I started to wish they would find something wrong with me and I would be exempt from service. I admit that I did not want to be in the military service. I had never been attracted to weapons, violence, or the idea of killing another person. On the other hand my sense of duty told me that I had to abide by the laws of the country where I now lived and would remain until my own country would be free again. Freedom has a price.

Another unsettling issue in my mind could be summarized by this question: Should I risk my life and/or lose it to save Vietnam from communism when I could be doing it for my own country just 90 miles away? Most Cubans, including me, could not figure out why the U.S. would go to faraway places to help those who needed help gaining freedom and democracy, and Cuba being so close had been forgotten by all. One day maybe we would know the answer to this question. Back in those days, I still had hope that the U.S. would help us regain our freedom. I obviously guessed incorrectly.

Many young men during those years were remaining in college or going to college to avoid the draft. Others were leaving the country or hiding in Canada to also avoid the war. I was not going to college and I was not leaving the U.S., so if I passed the physical exam, I was resigned to my destiny and I hoped that God had a good reason for me to go into the military. As expected, I passed the physical and I was classified 1-A, which meant I was at the front of the line to be drafted. One week later I received the draft notice that said: "Greetings! You are hereby ordered to report October 23, 1965 to the U.S. Army."

My parents, especially my mother, took the news very hard. The idea I could go to war was something they were not ready to deal with. They had sacrificed everything to take my sisters and me out of Cuba to free us from communism and to prevent me from serving in the Cuban militia, and now they were being faced with the reality that their son was going to war. The rest of the family was also concerned and worried when they found out. Yolanda was also worried and felt somewhat responsible. I assured her that she had actually helped me do the right thing.

Concern and worry was felt by all of us. We were concerned about the immediate future and the uncertainty of things to come impregnated our thoughts. I felt, scared, but also assured in my mind that God was in control. If this event would have taken place before I had found Christ in Cursillo, just a little over a year before, my outlook and behavior would have been totally different and a deeper sense of desperation and anger would have invaded my soul. Instead I prayed that the anxiety and sadness that I was feeling would serve as an offering to God so that, with His guidance, this new phase of my life would give glory to His name and would make me a better Christian and a better man.

Fortunately my parents had also attended Cursillo and were now practicing Catholics. We had several conversations discussing the issues and tried to discern how we needed to react to my going to war. Having surrendered the control to God did not totally take away the fears, anxieties, and trepidations, but it gave us the strength to keep these feelings at bay knowing that whatever was ahead was going to be for the greater good. Not only did I remain scared, but I also felt very uncomfortable with the anticipated duties and actions I was expected to perform as a soldier.

In my limited knowledge of soldiering, I realized that, as a soldier, I would be more exposed to danger and anguish than if I were to enlist in other branches of the military. I then decided to go to the Air Force recruiting office and tried to volunteer and enlist in the Air Force. I would have to serve four years instead of two, but I would have generally been in considerably less danger given that, by enlisting, you could choose what area and assignment you wanted.

The officer at the Air Force recruiting office was happy to see me and when I told him of my intentions he asked me where I was born. When I told him Cuba, he asked for my green card (which by the way was not green but blue, at that time). I told him I did not have one because I was a refugee under a parole and a waiver visa. The officer explained to me that in order to enlist, I needed to be a permanent resident or a citizen and that a Cuban refugee was not allowed to enlist. Disappointed I remarked: "You can be drafted, but you cannot enlist. Was that fair?" I then accepted the fact that I was going to be a soldier in the U.S. Army and that I would most likely be sent to war in Vietnam. May God help me! I thought.

On October 22, 1965 family members and close friends gathered at our house in west Hialeah to say our goodbyes. The next day I was to take a train to Fort Jackson, South Carolina (near Columbia, the capital of South Carolina). Needless to say it was a very emotional experience. My mother was trying to be strong, as she had always been, but I could see in her eyes the signs of profound anguish and fear. My father as always was trying to be funny, but his eyes could not hide the tears he was holding back trying to repress his anxiety through the use of humor.

Before that eventful day Yolanda and I had spent a lot of time alone trying to comfort each other and discussing our future plans. We had been talking about getting married in December, but now those plans were placed on hold until we knew what the immediate future had in store for us. We promised to write each other frequently and that often I would call collect from a pay-phone whenever I was able to. (No cellular phones then!) I could see in her tender eyes her love for me and her strength based on her never-yielding faith in God. She gave me courage and helped me trust that everything would be fine.

Early the next morning most of my family accompanied me to the train station in Miami. We said our goodbyes, kissed and hugged Cuban style. Cubans have this ritual of kissing and hugging when they arrive and when they leave any event. Sometimes the kissing and the hugging take longer than the event. I gave Yolanda a long and heartfelt kiss and a very close and passionate hug and then climbed on the train for the beginning of a journey into an unknown and uncertain future.

Chapter Seventeen
The U.S. Army Part One:
Basic Training

The train ride from Miami to Fort Jackson, South Carolina was long and boring. Most of those around me were also inductees into the Army. We did not know each other and given the mood, did not engage in much interaction or conversation. As I looked around I saw a cross section of the population of young men and I questioned how many of these, including me, would make it back from the war. I also wondered if I was going to get to know any of them better, or if we would serve together or die together.

After the end of the train ride, we were transported in buses to the Reception Station at Fort Jackson. At Fort Jackson we were "greeted" by a group of non-commission officers (NCOs). This is a designation given to those in position of leadership that are not officers such as corporals or sergeants. These NCOs proceeded to scream at us all sorts of instructions. Most of the group and I were so confused and frightened by their hostile attitudes that we acted and moved in the opposite direction of what their commands required. That provoked even more screams, insults, and threats. I thought that this welcome committee was very unreasonable because we did not know anything about the Army and its ways, but these NCOs expected that we react and move as if we had been trained already. This episode was just the beginning of all the nonsensical things we would encounter in the service.

I later found out that this area was called "Reception Station." That was some reception we got, but the manner in which we were treated persisted throughout the three days we were there. During those three days the inductees were grouped in platoons and marched (run would be a better description) by a leader called Roster Guide to the different stations in order to complete the process of induction before the basic training would begin.

The "deluxe" Reception Station tour consisted of getting a very short haircut, receiving several inoculations, "selecting" our new "wardrobe" (olive green), taking a battery of written tests, and having a lot of idle time used by the Roster Guide to make us march to nowhere. This marching activity repeated throughout the training phase many times over. The tour also included visits to the "Mess Hall." This is Army terminology for the cafeteria or food establishment. At the Mess Hall we would get three square meals a day. This was my favorite activity. As many people who know me well know, I love food and I loved Army food. It was all you could eat, as long as you ate it all in the allotted time. Everything was fresh and well prepared. They offered a variety of foods at all three meals. My favorites were breakfast and the desserts.

After successfully surviving these three days at the Reception Station, I was driven by bus to Fort Gordon, Georgia (Near Augusta) to the training company (Company D, First Battalion, First Brigade D-1-1) where I was going to have basic training with 102 other trainees. The next eight weeks turned out to be the most difficult, challenging, and demanding eight weeks of my life, even to this day. I had been told how difficult basic training was, but all of that was a plain and simple gigantic understatement of mammoth proportions. From the time I stepped out of the bus to the final graduation parade, I became the most insignificant creature on earth. My fellow trainees and I were told time and time again that we were below whale excrement (not the actual word used) as far as our superiors were concerned.

The Army's aim is to destroy all your self-esteem, self-importance, and all the good things you thought you were. By brining you down to the bottom of the ocean, actually below the bottom of the ocean, the Army can then build you up "the Army way." Our First Sergeant told us that there were three ways of doing something: the right way, the wrong way, and the Army way. He affirmed that from then on we would do anything the Army way or else. This also meant: doing extra pushups, extra running laps, extra turns in peeling potatoes, or corporal and mental punishment even jail time and dishonorable discharges.

My physical condition left a lot to be desired for my age. I was overweight and had not done any serious exercise in years. The first weeks of Basic I had a hard time keeping up with the rest of the trainees during all the physical demands of the training. During those first weeks I was also given the results of the battery of tests that I had taken. I was told I did very well and that I had qualified to take the aptitude test to enter Officer Candidate School (OCS). That really surprised me because I was never good at school or at taking tests. Even though I did not see myself as officer material, I took the test and passed it. I was then asked if I wanted to go to OCS after my advanced training. There were several options I considered at the time:

After successfully completing Basic I was to be sent to Advanced Infantry Training (AIT) for 8 weeks at Fort Jackson

South Carolina to participate in a special training designed for candidates to OCS and volunteers for Viet Nam. I had to also successfully complete AIT.

After AIT I was to be sent to Fort Benning, Georgia for the ten month OCS training. It was said to be ten times harder than Basic and AIT combined.

After successfully completing OCS I would get an officer commission of Second Lieutenant and serve for two years. This meant that my two original years of service as a draftee would become almost three.

The decision facing me was a pivotal one. After careful consideration, I decided to accept this honor and I signed up for OCS. Here is the logic that I used to make this extremely crucial decision:

My chances of going to the war zone were pretty high. If was going to go to war, I thought it would be better to do it as an officer rather than an NCO. Later I found out that this logic was full of holes (no pun intended) because Second Lieutenants as a group had the highest casualty rate in Vietnam because the Viet-Con snipers would shoot them first.

If I was going to be in the Army, why not be the best that I could be. This is a working philosophy that I have used throughout my life.

There were too many obstacles in the way and many successes I had to have in the way, so that maybe I would not attain all or some of them. In the meantime the original two-year commitment clock was running.

To further help me with the decision I ultimately and instinctively made, I used, without really knowing, what is called, Sensitivity Analysis. This tool uses three possible scenarios: best scenario, worst scenario, and, the most likely scenario. If the decision works with the worst scenario, you go for it. If it only works with the best, you do not go for it, and if it works with the most likely scenario you have a hard time deciding.

In my case the worst scenario presented two possibilities: Do not go to OCS, I am sent to war, and get killed; and the other go to OCS, finish it, go to war, and get killed. The decision did not work with the worst scenario. My best scenario was to graduate OCS, go to war, and come back alive. This one worked. My most likely scenario could be that I go to OCS and something happens and I do not make it to the end. If that happened, I would go back to the two year commitment and maybe the time left would not be enough for me to be sent to war. My decision only worked with the best or most likely, so it was hard to make.

Now that I was officially a candidate for OCS, I was made squad leader of the fourth squad of my training platoon. I was given the temporary rank of corporal. As a squad leader the expectations were much higher if I was to retain that position, so now my physical conditioning became more of an issue. I was lucky that a member of my squad was the top trainee for the Physical Training (PT) Test we did the first week and because I was one of the last to finish it, I asked him to help me train better after hours. I was to take this test again at the end of the eight weeks and if I did not pass it, I would be recycled and I had to do Basic all over again. If this was not enough motivation, I also would be dropped from OCS. My fellow trainee helped me improve my running speed and my ability to negotiate the infamous "Monkey Bars." We worked very hard, and I was getting better every day. The fact that I was also losing a lot of weight also helped. I lost 40 pound in eight weeks.

During these eight weeks I was trained shooting an M-14 rifle (Do not ever, ever call it a gun. If you did, the sergeant would publicly humiliate you by pointing at the rifle and then to a certain part of his anatomy while saying: "This is a rifle and this is a gun. One is for battle, the other for fun." After that you were punished by being forced to do any number of push-ups with your rifle laid on top of your hands), throwing a live hand grenade, hand-to-hand combat, ballonet combat assault, first aid, target detection, gas mask use, and the most difficult and nerve racking exercise of all: we had to crawl under a barbwire while a machine gun fired live ammunition "whistling" above our heads. We had to do it twice, once during the day and the other one at night where they used tracers. (Tracers are bullets with a tip that lights up after it is fired). To make it even harder for us, the night we had to do this training, it rained a lot. Because of the rain, we were crawling in the mud. When I finished, I had mud in places of my body, that would be embarrassing to describe.

Chapter Eighteen
The U.S. Army Part Two:
Christmas Leave. Wedding Plans

My Basic Training was progressing well, and I was getting the hang of military discipline and life. We were told that during Christmas we would have eight days of leave and that we were to come back to end the training. Then we would have two weeks of leave before we were to report to our next training. That was good news and it motivated me even more to try to finish with a good record. One of those lonely nights before we went to sleep, I was lying in bed thinking of Yolanda, how much I missed her and how much I would love to marry her as we had planned before I was drafted. The following week was going to be my 22nd birthday and we had agreed in one of our letter exchanges that I would call her (collect), so she could wish me happy birthday.

I said to myself: "Why not get married as planned? What is stopping us? For one, I was not making enough money to support a wife on the trainee's salary of $87.90 per month. The minimum wage that year was $1.25, which for a 40-hour week translated to $217.00 per month. The Army paid less because we were given housing, medical care, laundry services, and food. If you look at it considering these extras, we were well paid, but still not enough to support a wife. Another consideration was, where would we live. After finishing training, I could live with her off-post and the Army would pay me and extra $55.70 per month, but that meant that I could not eat at the Mess Hall anymore. There were two situations to consider: One, if I we got married before I finished the training, we could not live together until I finished AIT, and two, if we waited until I finished training we would not have enough money to pay rent and food ($87.90 + $55.70 = $143.60) considerably below the minimum wage.

The night before my birthday was Sunday and we had had a light day of training, but Monday, the day of my birthday we were scheduled for a forced march of 10 miles. As I was trying to sleep, I was praying for God to give me guidance. I made the decision that the next night I would ask Yolanda to marry me. This was my plan:

I would use the five-day leave for Christmas from December 19 to December 23 to get married. I would arrive via train in Miami December 19 in the evening. We would be married December 20 (Monday). She would have to make all the arrangements in 42 days.

After the wedding, we would both drive north from Miami, in her 1964 Plymouth Valiant for a mini-honeymoon which would have us in Fort Gordon by December 26.

Yolanda would drive from Fort Gordon to Savannah Georgia (approximately 2.5 hours and 127 miles) to stay with my cousin Tavito and his family until December 30 when I would finish Basic Training.

Yolanda would drive to Fort Gordon on December 30 to pick me up and we would then continue on a real honeymoon for two weeks.

On January 15 I was to report to Fort Jackson South Carolina for AIT. I would travel by train and Yolanda would stay in Miami working at her current job until further notice.

When I dropped the proposal on my phone conversation, all I heard was a prolonged silence. I said: "¿Me oístes?" (Did you hear me?) Yolanda told me yes, I heard you. She then said: "How am I to prepare a wedding in 42 days?" Well, I said, do you want to marry me or not? She said yes and I said, "Everything else is secondary. Do the best you can." I then told her my plan for after the wedding and she agreed. The only thing left was to get permission from the Army to get married during training. After talking to several of my superiors who tried to talk me out of it, my Captain gave me permission but not without a lecture about what would happen if I got killed in Vietnam.

When I spoke to my parents later that night, I told them of my wedding plans I got another lecture about what would happen if I get killed in the war. I told them that first I was not going to get killed, and second if I did she would just continue to work and collect the death benefit from the Army, a benefit of $10,000. After everyone knew that the decision was made, they all jumped on board and helped us make it happen.

The idea that I was going to be married was an added motivation for me to do well and finish my training. The weeks did not pass quickly enough and my physical conditioning was improving as I was losing weight almost every week even though I was eating lots of food. The constant exercise and the stress that I had were responsible for my improved performance. The time came for the Christmas leave, and I took the bus down to Miami with my heart full of happiness and positive expectations for the future.

Chapter Nineteen
The U.S. Army Part Three:
The Wedding.
Back to training. Mini Honeymoon

As I arrived at the bus terminal in downtown Miami, my heart was racing faster than ever. I could not wait to see Yolanda. I had not seen her since she went with her mother to my cousin's house in Savannah during one of my weekend passes. Now I was going to see her and kiss her, but with the added bonus that I was going to marry her the following day. It was a Sunday and downtown Miami was almost deserted. As the bus pulled into the station, I saw her with her mother and my parents. She looked as pretty as ever. I felt at that moment I was the luckiest guy in the world.

Everything had been set up for the wedding at Saint John Bosco Catholic Church on Flagler Street and 13th Avenue in Miami. This was Yolanda's parish and as the tradition goes, the Sacrament of Matrimony should be administered at the bride's parish. Our wedding was to take place on Monday December 20, 1965 at 8:00 PM. I had not heard of anyone, nor have ever I since, of someone getting married on a Monday at the church. Most of the time weddings take place on Fridays or Saturdays.

Saint John Bosco Catholic Church stood as a symbol for the Cuban exiles. Its pastor, Father Emilio Vallina, was very close to Yolanda and was a great supporter of the Cursillos movement. The building where the church was housed had been a warehouse that the bishop had acquired and Father Vallina and his parishioners had adapted it into a church. It was not what you called a traditional-looking Catholic church, but it had a hidden charisma you could sense every time you visited it. Yolanda was a very active parishioner of San Juan Bosco, as it was called, and she had arranged all the details with Father Vallina. She even got permission from him for Father Miguel de Arrillaga, the head of Cursillos, to be the principal celebrant in the wedding Mass. This was the priest who told me to stay away from Yolanda a few years before.

There was one problem with the structure of the church building that Yolanda needed to change. The main entrance to the church did not lead to the center aisle. It had two doors to each side of a wall that was built between the entrance door and the center aisle. The brides that had been married there before, had to go in the door, then come in from the side to the center aisle in order to proceed down the center aisle to the altar. A couple of weeks after she got the word that we were going to be married, she went to Father Vallina and asked him to change the entrance by removing that obstructing wall and making a clearer passage from the entrance door to the center aisle. At first Father Vallina hesitated, but in order to please his very good parishioner and member of the leadership of Cursillos, he agreed to do it. The fact that Yolanda softly insinuated that she would have to go to another parish might have had something to do with his decision too.

Father Vallina contacted his good friends and ours, Francisco (Paquito) Delgado and Armando Alejandre, who were Cursillistas, and who had helped Father Vallina with the remodeling of the church. Paquito was a general contractor and Alejandre was a Cuban architect whom I had given a ride to one time to Saint Michael's church for his Cursillo. As a side note, Alejandre was the father of Armando Alejandre junior, one of the four Cubans that were killed by Cuban communist planes as they shot down the Brothers to the Rescue planes in international waters in 1996. This crime was never prosecuted by the U.S. ,the UN, or any of the so-called human rights organizations. This terrorist act was also virtually ignored by the worldwide press. Our friends Paquito and Alejandre made the changes to San Juan Bosco and Yolanda and all the other brides thereafter, were able to enter the church in a more elegant and ceremonial manner.

The ceremony was to be simple and the bridal party was composed of some of the members of both families. Given that Yolanda's dad, Jose Eustacio Marcos, had died in a traffic accident in Cuba before Yolanda came to Miami, her very good friend and supervisor at the Welfare Department, Guillermo Vargas, a devout Cursillista, was to walk her down the aisle and was our Best Man. The Matron of Honor was going to be my mother Pepa. All our family members were invited as well as all our friends including those from Añorada Cuba, Cursillos, and the Welfare Department.

As far as the wedding reception, Yolanda had obtained permission to use the parish center at Saint Peter and Paul parish nearby. She had also contacted the members of my former band, Conjunto Tropical, and they had agreed to play for free. At the reception we would have cake and Spanish Cider (Similar to Champagne) and some "saladitos." It was to be a very simple reception. Overall Yolanda had done a fabulous job putting all of these and other details together in only 42 days. These days, brides seem to "need" at least a year to organize a "proper" wedding. Go figure!

Yolanda's wedding gown was beautiful. She had borrowed it from a close friend and had made some alterations on it. I would be wearing my Army Class A uniform. My soon to be brother-in-law Pupy, my sister Pepita's boyfriend, was going to drive Yolanda to the church, and both of us to the reception in a big car he borrowed from his car business. He also helped me hide Yolanda's 1964 Plymouth Valiant in a secret location where my friends could not find it to "decorate it." He could drive us to that location after the reception, and we could drive to our first night of the honeymoon in peace.

Everything was ready, but I felt reassured that Yolanda was meant to be my wife and mother of my children, I was 100% sure of what I was doing; Yolanda was ready as well. Yolanda and I were also sure that God had put us together and that we would be together forever. We both had some trepidation about our immediate future, but we had none as far as our love for each other was concerned. With God's Grace that we would receive in the Sacrament of Matrimony, we would be able to accept whatever was in store for us. We had both surrendered to Christ and the Holy Spirit and had given control to God.

The wedding was beautiful and Father Miguel's sermon touched all of us there. He knew us very well and especially Yolanda, so he was able to give a heartfelt homily that inspired us all. The Mass was done with all the rituals and because the congregation was mainly composed of practicing Catholics, the participation in the prayers, songs, and especially in Communion, was outstanding. I believe all those Communions that were offered for us by our family and friends have been an important part of our marriage persevering. Those prayers and Communions had been our "reserve tank." This spiritual reserve we had to use many times when our own "tank' seemed to be running low. This was a blessed event and you could feel the presence of the Holy Spirit throughout the ceremony.

The reception was also very nice and simple. We took lots of pictures and everyone had a good time. The music was very good. Wedding receptions must have good music to be successful (This is an extremely biased opinion). The parish center at Saint Peter and Paul was filled to capacity. We received lots of presents and especially lots of blessings and good wishes from all of those there. The time came for Yolanda and I to depart and many of my friends were conspiring to "adorn" our car for the honeymoon, but they could not find it. Yolanda and I changed our clothes at the reception and we left in Pupy's car. He made some evasive maneuvers and took different back streets until we lost all of those pursuing us. We reached Yolanda's car, and I drove it to the destination of our first night together in North Miami Beach.

We stayed at a hotel called the Castaways; it is no longer there, but it was located on A1A and 163rd Street in the Northeast section of Miami Dade County. This was a beautiful hotel with good rooms and it was perfect for a first honeymoon night. Yolanda was very nervous of course, and I was happier than I had ever felt in my life. When I opened the door of the room, I carried her in my arms across the threshold, and brought her into the room. The rest of what happened will not be discussed in detail for obvious reasons. Suffice it to say that our first night more than fulfilled my expectations and was the culmination of the greatest day of my life.

The next morning after breakfast we proceeded up the coast driving up A1A all the way until, after several days, we entered Georgia, and then we proceeded to Atlanta where Yolanda's sister, Ondina, her daughter, Ondinita, and

Ondina's husband Ricardo Garcia-Menocal, a very well known sports writer in Cuba, lived. We spent a few days in Atlanta celebrating Christmas Eve and Christmas with them. On December 26 Yolanda left me at Fort Gordon in order for me to finish my Basic Training, and she proceeded to Savannah, to stay with my cousin Tavito and his family until the end of my training December 30th.

In these five days I was to take the infamous PT test and finish all the other requirements for graduation. I was successful in the PT test and passed the two events that I had failed in the initial assessment. My mile run time came down from over 11 minutes to 7 minutes; I was able to negotiate, very slowly, the monkey bars. The graduation ceremony was very simple and short, and all of us said our goodbyes to each other and wished each other a safe and successful advanced training.

Chapter Twenty
The U.S. Army Part Four:
Honeymoon
Advanced Infantry Training

Yolanda picked me up at Fort Gordon and we headed south to Miami making several stops along the way. Cypress Gardens and Silver Spring were among the attractions that we enjoyed while enjoying each other's company. We had only two weeks to be together, but these two weeks were unforgettable as we were getting to know each other better and learning more about each other. After a few days we got to Miami and decided to rent an apartment for the rest of the days I was going to be there.

Yolanda was not trained in the homemaker activities because when she lived with her mother and cousin, she was working full time and devoted all her extra time to the Church and Cursillos. I knew that since we first started going out and after we became engaged; besides had proof positive of that when Yolanda, while we were engaged, asked me to dinner at her home. She told me; "I am going to cook for you your favorite food. Tell me what it is, so I can make it for you." I was aware of her lack of training in this area and tried to come up with something that would be easy to cook. I said: "I love 'tortilla de platanos maduros'" (Ripe plantain omelet). How hard can this be? I said to myself. She set a date and I was looking forward to it. It was going to be the first meal she would prepare for me.

The day came and I showed up at her home to be greeted by her mom and her cousin Terina. They told me to sit down and that Yolanda was cooking for me. While I was waiting, Terina went to the kitchen to check on Yolanda's progress. Terina was an experienced cook and wanted to see if Yolanda needed help. All of a sudden I hear Terina laughing loud in the kitchen. I was not told at the time why they were laughing, but I learned it later that evening. When Terina entered the kitchen she found that Yolanda had done a good job breaking and beating the eggs, peeling and cutting the plantains, and setting the oil in the frying pan. As Terina continued to observe she saw Yolanda putting the raw plantain pieces into the raw beaten eggs. In order to make this omelet, you must first deep-fry the plantains, and then put them in the beaten eggs; otherwise, they will not cook as fast as the eggs and the omelet would be ruined.

Now that we were married and living temporarily under the same roof, she wanted to cook for me again. Yolanda is a very smart woman and she is also very persistent. She impressed me with those qualities from the first days of our marriage. She went to the store and bought some "palomilla" steaks, rice, canned vegetables, and Cuban bread. She announced that she was making steaks with vegetable rice as a side dish. She also told me that she did not want my help, knowing that I had cooked before when I was in Los Angeles. I stayed away from the kitchen area and anxiously awaited her masterpiece.

The steaks were great and cooked medium as I like them, but the rice was, shall I say, not up to par. She had cooked the rice and then she had mixed it up with the can vegetables and had forgotten to put some "bijol" (food coloring). The vegetable rice in the Cuban cuisine is supposed to be yellow and the vegetables are cooked as you cook the rice so, the rice will get the flavor of the vegetables. She presented me with her creation and I told her it was great. I even had seconds. She later found out what she had done, not from me of course, and this event has always been used by both of us in a humorous manner. Yolanda, through the years has become an excellent homemaker and her cooking is superb in every aspect, proof of her tenacity and love for her family and me.

Those few days that we spent in our temporary nest, were wonderful and laid the foundation that would hold our marriage together for so many years. The day came that I had to get back to "Uncle Sam's Army" and we had to say goodbye for a while. I took the bus to Fort Jackson, South Carolina to begin my AIT for the next eight weeks. It was very hard to leave Yolanda in Miami, but there was nothing I could do. We promised to write very frequently (Boy, we could have used, emails, texting, and Skype). We talked on the phone at least once a week. My parents were also concerned for my future. My mother was very sad and I later found out, that she was praying all the time. God, through the graces of Cursillo, had given her the peace and trust that she needed to face her son's facing the possibility of not making it back alive. My father, who was more positive, took this a little better using humor to hide his true feelings.

I arrived at Fort Jackson in early January 1966 and reported to Company D-11-3 housed in Fort Gordon, in World War II era barracks, in the hills of South Carolina. The training was hard, but it felt easier than basic mainly because we were all in top physical condition and by then most of us had adapted to the rigors of military life. Our company was composed of two groups of trainees: those like me, candidates to OCS and those who had enlisted in the Army and asked to be sent to the war. Needless to say that most of us were motivated to learn well and pass this training given our future trajectory. The design of the training was also different than a regular AIT because the Army needed to make sure that we would be ready when we would get to Vietnam because that was our destination.

We were trained in most of the infantry weapons such as bazookas, grenade launchers, M-30 and M-50 machine guns, 45 caliber pistol, as well as advanced target detection and hand-to-hand combat training. Part of the training took place inside of a make-believe Vietnam village that they had constructed with booby-traps and all, in the wooded area of the fort. We also had a very intense physical training that included long tactical marches and lots of running.

As the training progressed, I was getting more and more scared of the certainty that I was going to war. I am not ashamed of confessing that the reality of our training made me feel at times that I was already in Vietnam. I used to have nightmares about it. I could only imagine what the real thing would do to me. As the training progressed, I felt more and more like a robot. The effectiveness of the training had replaced my personal feelings and principles with those that the Army wanted and needed me to have when I would be faced with war. I felt as they kept repeating to us: "you are a lean and mean killing machine." Was I brainwashed? Maybe, but not totally.

Many nights as I tried to go to sleep, thoughts of Yolanda invaded me. Many nights I dreamed about her and those beautiful eyes looking at me and telling me how much she loved me. These experiences later gave birth to a song that I wrote a few months later called: "Sueño de un Soldado." (A Soldier's Dreams). Here are the Spanish lyrics:

Ya las luces se han apagado
En la barraca ya son las diez
Y en la cama está acostado
Y en ella piensa atormentado
Soledad la del soldado
Que por las noches hasta ha llorado
Y en la mañana muy temprano
Se levanta el soldado
Y muy triste y acongojado
El verá que ella no está a su lado
Todo era un sueño, oh, oh
Un sueño de soldado, oh, oh
Un sueño de soldado

An English translation of the song:

All the lights were out
In the barracks, it is already ten
And in the bed already laying
Thinking of her with torment
Loneliness of the soldier
Who at night has even cried
And in the morning very early
The soldier gets up
And very sad and sorrowful
He sees she is not at his side
Everything was a dream, oh, oh
A soldier's dream, oh. Oh
A soldier's dream

I would call Yolanda several times per week and we would tell each other how much we loved each other. Those few weeks that we were apart seemed like years.

An announcement was made that on the fifth weekend of our 8-week training we would get a three-day pass. For the Army a three-day pass is actually from Saturday morning until Sunday night. Last time I checked that is just two days, but that is the "Army Way." This was great news for me because right away I called Yolanda to make arrangements to fly to Columbia, South Carolina on Friday night and fly back to Miami on Sunday afternoon. That would give us a few hours together, which we both longed for. Yolanda agreed and I went into town the next chance I had made a reservation at a motel called Laurel Motel. Yolanda would take a taxi to the motel and wait for my arrival early Saturday morning.

That Saturday morning we got up really early as usual and before we were dismissed for the so called three-day pass, the first sergeant wanted to see how badly we wanted this pass, so he ordered the training sergeant to take us for a run. Everyone was upset to see how they were playing with us and putting us through yet another harassing exercise. I was determined to run as long as I needed in order for my plans to come through. We started with a run around the exercise field, approximately 3 miles. As we were approaching the starting point, the trainer said: "Let's go around one more time."

Several of my fellow trainees dropped out half way through in a sign of frustration. Many of us continued on. As we were approaching the starting point for the second time, the training sergeant said: "Let's see who among you really wants to go on the pass." As he said that many dropped out, but not me. We went like one quarter of a mile; then, the training sergeant said; "Okay, that is enough." and took us back. He wanted to see how many would give up thinking that they had to go around a third time.

Given that most of the company dropped out, the first sergeant cancelled the pass. I was so upset and angry at this unfair practice that I decided I was going to town no matter what. I started to plan that I would go after lights out and sneak out of the fort. This act is called: going AWOL or Absent Without Leave and it is a punishable act that carried severe consequences. When I knew that Yolanda was already there, I called the motel and told her what was happening. She told me not to risk it, but I did not listen. The combination of my Cuban and Basque hardheadedness took over and I felt betrayed and treated unfairly and I was not going to stand for it.

As lights went out, I told two of my fellow trainees, the ones that slept on either side of my bed, what I was going to do. They helped me put pillows under my covers to simulate my body and then I snuck out of the company grounds toward the area where the taxis were parked waiting for the soldiers to go to town. I got in the taxi and told the driver what I was doing. At first he did not want to do it, but when I offered him $20 up front and another $20 when he would pick me up at 4 AM, he agreed to do it. I was hidden in the back seat when he went through the gates and I got to Laurel Motel and stayed with Yolanda all night. At 4 AM the taxi picked me up and I was back in my bed when reveille sounded at 5 AM. I felt great!

As we went to the morning formation, we were informed that passes would be given starting Sunday morning for one day. I then got myself together and took a taxi to the Laurel Motel. This time I did so legally. We spent the whole day together and I took her in a taxi to the airport where we said our goodbyes. During this episode Yolanda and I received the precious gift from God of our first daughter Yolanda Maria who was born 9 months after that weekend.

The rest of training was nothing compared to this experience. I was able to finish it and graduate. A big question mark still loomed: "What was waiting for me on the horizon as I waited for my orders?"

Chapter Twenty One
The U.S. Army Part Five:
The first biggest decision
of my military career

Right after the graduation ceremony, when we got back to the company area, everyone got orders, except me. Those who were scheduled to go to OCS were talking about it and looking forward to the tremendous challenge ahead of them in Fort Benning, Georgia. Those who had volunteered to go to the war in Vietnam were also excited and believe it or not, happy that they could go there and serve their country. I, Private Rolando M. Ochoa was very confused and scared because I had not received my orders to go to OCS.

To clarify my status I decided to go see my Company Commander to get some answers. He told me that he had little information and that I had to go and see the Brigade G2 because there was some problem with my security clearance. The G2 (Same designation given by Castro to the macabre ministry of intelligence in Cuba) was the section in charge of security and intelligence. As I was walking toward that building a few minutes from my company, many thoughts were running through my head. Had the Army decided not to send me to OCS because I was a Cuban refugee with no permanent status? Would I be sent to Vietnam right away given my training? Had they found out something in my past or maybe were mistaking me for someone else and decided to cancel my OCS training? The level of stress was increasing by the second and as I reached the G2 office, I was ready for the worst.

After waiting for a few minutes (which seemed like hours) I met with the Colonel who was the G2. He was a very tall and distinguished soldier of about 50 years of age or so. As I approached his desk I saw a blank expression on his face. He had a neutral expression typical of officers who had gone through so many difficult experiences. I saluted him and was asked to sit down at his desk. He had my file on his desk. He opened it and then looked at me straight in the eyes and said: "Private Ochoa you have a problem and a decision to make." I felt like my soul had escaped from my body, and I was sure my heart had stopped. "Private Ochoa, he proceeded, your security clearance papers, which were started when you first entered the Army, have been lost. Without this clearance, you cannot go to OCS. Given that you are a refugee (here we go, I thought) the process is longer than usual, and it would take at least 4 more months to finalize it. You have two choices: Wait for the security clearance process to be done again and then, if successful, go to OCS, or you can resign OCS and then wait for your other orders. I must have your decision now."

How can they lose my papers? I thought. How could he ask me to make such a decision without time to think about it? I then put myself together and thought: If I resign from OCS, I will, for sure, get orders to Vietnam and be there within a week, so that choice was out. I then told the colonel: "You are really telling me that I have one choice. I will wait for the security clearance." He wrote something in my file and asked me to report to the Reception Center Company where I would spend my time working until I would get the security clearance.

After I left, I gave this dilemma more thought. The more I thought about it, the better I felt about the decision. I was now in the Army for 4 months. Four more months waiting would make it 8 months. If I were to go to OCS training, it would be 10 months making it 18 out of the required 24 months of my draft. Assuming I would not make it through OCS, that would leave me less than the 13 months minimum tour of duty in Viet-Nam, so I would not be sent. If I were to make it through OCS, I would be sent to Viet Nam as a Second Lieutenant and my time in the Army would be almost 3 years instead of the original 2 years of the draft. I then found the nearest telephone and called Yolanda to tell her what had happened.

This event created additional stress and anxiety in our already difficult marital situation. I found myself away from Yolanda who was expecting our first child and confused about what our immediate future would be like. Our love for each other kept us united, strong, and committed to make the marriage work and to give our first child the best possible life. We spoke on the phone quite frequently and continued to write letters to each other.

Shortly after, I reported to my new "temporary" unit and was assigned the duties of a Roster Guide at the reception station. I was somewhat familiar with the job because when I was inducted to the Army, I had spent the first few days at the same reception station and experienced the rigors provided by the system and by the roster guides who drove the recruits without mercy through processing. Now it was I who had to drive the inductees hard and without mercy. An experienced roster guide worked with me for the cycle of three days so I could learn the "trade." After that I was on my own.

Because I spoke Spanish, they used to give me the platoon where most of the Puerto Ricans were placed. The Army was drafting a lot of Puerto Rican nationals at the time and a lot of them did not know how to speak English. The experience of the reception station was bad enough, but not understanding what the roster guides were saying, made it even worse. I spoke to them in English for the first two days. This was done, so they would experience the discipline and the rigors of the first few days of the Army. It was also done because I did not want them to think that because I spoke Spanish, they could get away with not doing things as they were mandated to do. I needed their respect and obedience and I thought that if I spoke Spanish they would take advantage of me.

The tactic worked because I taught them drill exercises and other things they could use in basic training. On the last day, I spoke to them in Spanish and they were delighted. I took that opportunity to instill in them a sense of pride and challenged them to be the best platoon in the company. Most of them reacted favorably to that idea, and I was many times congratulated by my superiors for how well my platoon could march and do other exercises. After a while I was promoted to Private First Class (PFC), which carried a grade of E-3 with a little more money in my pay.

Because of my promotion, I requested permission to bring my wife to the fort and live "off-post." This meant that I would not live in the barracks, but in my own place outside the fort with my wife. This was a big decision because Yolanda would have to quit her job that was supporting her in Miami, and we both had to live with the $85 per month salary plus an allowance for food of $35 per month. Out of that very small income, we would have to pay for our living expenses, food, and her car payment of $50 per month.

We knew it would be tough, but the desire to be together and our strong commitment to each other outweighed all the logic and advice that we got from many around us. I found a place to live just outside one of the gates in a trailer park where we rented a very small trailer for $50 per month all included. Our first home was not what most of us dreamed of, but that was all we could afford. It rested on tires and had some steps to climb in order to get in. The bathroom was so small that when I needed to use the toilet, my knees would push against the wall in front of it. It was not a pretty picture, but reality at the time.

In order to save money I bought a used bicycle at the thrift shop for $3 and I used it to go to work to save on gas. The food was a problem. Usually on the last week of the month (In the Army you get paid at the end of each month), we were out of money and out of food. This situation was solved by, I am afraid to say, breaking a few rules. Because I had separate rations and I was getting $35 per month, I was not supposed to eat at the Mess Hall (Dining Facility) where the rest of my company ate. So I would go to the Reception Center's Mess Hall where all the inductees had their meals and ate there risking getting caught, but I only did it when we needed it. Not only would I eat, but I would also take some food in my pockets to take to Yolanda.

Our next-door neighbors were a couple from Puerto Rico about our age. The wife was also expecting and the husband was a permanent cook at one of the training companies. There was a rule in the Army that the food was not kept from one day to the next and anything leftover was thrown away in the garbage. Other food that was perishable, like eggs, was also thrown away when the expiration date came about. Our guardian angel, our good Samaritan neighbor risking his own skin, would knock at our door at night and would give us a package containing whatever he could bring that day. We ate a lot of eggs in those days. Somehow we managed and we very happy together. Also Yolanda's niece, Ondinita, who lived in Atlanta, Georgia on many weekends would drive to Fort Jackson with her mother and father to visit us. They would always bring us food, which was the best present we could get. We were eternally grateful for that.

While we were in Fort Jackson, we started to go to Mass at Chapel 10 where they had a 12:15 PM Mass in Spanish. The majority of the congregation was Puerto Rican. The Mass was officiated by an Italian-America chaplain/priest named Father Evangelisto who spoke perfect Spanish and drove a scooter all over the fort. Father Evangelisto was a dedicated priest who worked many hours and was always there for the troops. We became friends almost immediately after we introduced ourselves to him after one Sunday Mass. I offered him my help in reading or singing at the Mass, which he gracefully accepted. God works in mysterious ways as you will soon see!

Chapter Twenty Two
The U.S. Army Part Six:
The second biggest decision of my military career

Yolanda and I were living sort of a normal married life during my time at the reception station, but I was always thinking of what would happen next, when the security clearance issue would be resolved. It was during one of those very quiet nights at the trailer park when I composed the song: "Sueño de un Soldado." (A Soldier's Dream) The idea for this song came from the time I was alone and in training. It was difficult financially, but we were very happy to be together during Yolanda's pregnancy. The Army doctors took good care of her every time she went in for a checkup even though she saw a different doctor on every visit. We started to meet other Army families at the Sunday Mass and made some friendships that have lasted until today.

Among these new friends was a wonderful lady named Gloria Fajardo who was the wife of Captain Jose Fajardo. Captain Fajardo was one of the heroes of the Bay of Pigs invasion of Cuba in 1961 who, among others, were given the opportunity to join the U.S. Army as officers. This offer was done as "repayment" for the catastrophe caused by President Kennedy's decision to withdraw support for the Cuban troops whot were trying to overthrow the communist regime after they were trained by the CIA. In my opinion, this has been one of the biggest errors ever made by any president. Gloria Fajardo was a very friendly and supportive person. She immediately took Yolanda under her wing and became her best friend and counselor. Gloria had two daughters; Glorita, almost nine years old and Rebecca, around 3 years old, who accompanied her to Mass every Sunday. Glorita became the extremely famous Gloria Estefan.

We later found out that there were a number other former Bay of Pig heroes in Fort Jackson. We were lucky to meet quite a few of them and become friends with many of them. One of my favorites was Captain Candido Molinet who was extremely outgoing and fun to be around. He and his wife Aida opened their home to us and were a great support during those trying times. We also met many Puerto Rican families. The husbands were in the regular Army. There were several young Cubans whom we also met at the Mass; some of them became close friends. "El Gato" Manuel Diaz, Guillermo Gafas, Luis Suarez, and Claudio Benedi and I became very close. We used to gather in Captain Molinet's home very often. Claudio Benedi became my closest friend because we had a lot in common. His wife Mery was also pregnant and he was also waiting for his security clearance to go to OCS.

One Sunday after Mass, Father Evangelisto asked me to wait for him because he needed to speak with me about something important. We waited and when he came out to talk to us outside Chapel 10 he said; "My assistant (Who was from Puerto Rico) just received orders to go to Vietnam and I need a new assistant. Do you want to be my assistant?" That came out of nowhere. This was a new ingredient to the already confusing equation of my military future. I did not know what to say. Sensing that I was in shock, Father Evangelisto proceeded to explain that what I needed to do was resign my OCS holdover status; then he would transfer me to his unit as a chaplain's assistant. If I were to receive orders within the first 90 days of the transfer, I would go to Viet-Nam as an infantry soldier. On the other hand if the orders would come after the 90 days, I would go as a chaplain's assistant, which was a "big" difference.

I looked at Yolanda. She was as confused as I was. Then I asked Father Evangelisto if we could think about it. He said yes, but that he did not have much time. We went home and talked and prayed about it. Was this a sign from God to save me from the war? Was this opportunity the "real" reason I was in the Army? Should I gamble with that, given the generalized confusion in my records that I would not get orders in less than 90 days? We slept on it and in the morning we decided to accept the offer and put ourselves in God's hands.

My first day as a chaplain's assistant was spent in the Post Chaplain's office located near the Fort Headquarters. There I met the Post Chaplain, the head of the assistants, and other members of the unit. The next day I was assigned to Chapel 15, I also would assist Father Evangelisto with the Spanish speaking troops and the Spanish Mass in Chapel 10. Chapel 15 was a multi-denominational Chapel while Chapel 10 was just a Catholic Chapel. At Chapel 15 there was no Catholic priest assigned, so I reported to the Baptist Chaplain. On Sunday a priest from another chapel would come to say Mass at 9:00 AM after setting up the chapel for a Catholic Mass; then at 10:00 AM the chapel was to be converted to a Protestant Chapel. The cycle was repeated for the 11:00 AM Mass and the 12:00 PM Protestant service. All these changes were executed by me and a senior Protestant Chaplain's assistant stationed at Chapel 15. Then at 12:15 I was at Chapel 10 for the Spanish Mass.

Both the Protestant chaplain and his assistant were great Christians. We became good friends. I fondly remember how we would have profound discussions about our differences, yet always in a very amicable and ecumenical manner. Across from Chapel 15 was the post Synagogue where the Jewish soldiers would go to worship on Saturdays. The rabbi was a young New Yorker with a keen sense of humor and a profound knowledge of the Old Testament. On occasions the three of us from Chapel 15 would go to the Synagogue and have a very animated religious discussion. I learned a lot from these individuals not the least of which was the ability to hear and respect different opinions and viewpoints.

During these very tense 90 days I trembled every time a communication would come to the office thinking that it contained my orders to go to Vietnam. Compounding my anxiety was the fact that Yolanda and I were new to the pregnancy experience and even though Yolanda was doing quite well, we still felt a sense of trepidation and anxiety all the time. I felt especially stressed when I thought of the possibility of being sent to war while Yolanda was left alone to deal with the birth of our first child. The contact with all those newfound friends and their support made the whole experience bearable.

Chapter Twenty Three
The U.S. Army Part Seven:
The "real reason" why I was drafted

Despite the training and the impending fear of going off to war, Army life was actually relatively easy as long as one stayed within the Army rules. As a permanent party (Army talk for assigned to a unit) and as a chaplain's assistant, I kept regular office hours during the week and only worked very hard on weekends while assisting in all the Masses and services assigned to me. I thought at the time that if I could stay where I was, I would even enjoy the experience. Besides I had the opportunity to help others in the worship of God and help some of the troops when they wanted to speak with the Chaplain for counseling and confession. On occasion I would also be used as a driver for the chaplains including the Post Chaplain whenever they needed to attend a graduation or a field Mass.

One day Father Evangelisto called me to his office. He related to me his concern with the level of religious preparation of the draftees from Puerto Rico. It seemed that many of them had not made their First Communion and even some of them had not even been baptized. He tried to counsel them when they came to see him, but there were just too many. He wanted to know if I could assume the responsibility to provide them with Catechism classes and prepare them for First Communion and Baptism. I told Father Evangelisto that I did not think I was qualified or prepared to do that and he told me that he thought I was, and that he would help me. I accepted this new challenge with a lot trepidation and asked God to help me. I also had the help of Yolanda who was a lot more prepared in religious instruction and topics than I was. Was this the reason why I was drafted? At the time I thought it was.

We then started to promote these classes at all the Masses and before we knew it, we had a large number of soldiers signed up. The process was to send a notification to every training company that had trainees signed up for the classes, so the company could give releases to the trainees for the religious training. The Army gives a lot of weight to the religious needs of its troops and Chaplains have a lot of influence. I personally delivered these requests to each of the companies' offices. In many of those deliveries the First Sergeant of that company was there to receive the requests. First Sergeants have a lot of influence and are for the most part tough and rough guys. On one of those occasions this First Sergeant proceeded to give me a hard time about it. He said: "Why do these trainees need to go to religious training. They are here to be trained for war, etc." I told him that I was just the delivery person and that I would communicate his concerns to my Chaplain. When I got back to the Father Evangelisto's office, I told him about this overly zealous First Sergeant. Father called the company to speak with him. When the First Sergeant got on the phone father said; "This is Captain Chaplain Evangelisto. I understand that you had some questions as to the reason why these troops need to come to religious training. Let me play Chaplain and you play First Sergeant." The First Sergeant only said: "Yes sir I will." After that every time I went to that company, the First Sergeant was very pleasant with me and never again gave me a hard time. The power of rank is very strong in the Army, but the power of the Chaplains was clearly even stronger.

The Catechism classes were going well and Yolanda and I were the godparents to the first group that was baptized. It took several weeks to prepare the group for their first communion. They went to their first confession with Father Evangelisto. Afterward he told me that we had done a good job in preparing them. All these activities kept me busy; however, my mind stayed preoccupied by the possible change of orders and the upcoming birth of our first child.

As expected the 90 days went by quickly, and I did not get orders to go to Vietnam. Now I could relax a little bit knowing that if I were to go to the war zone, it would be as an officially designated chaplain's assistant. Father Evangelisto recommended me for a promotion and I was soon promoted to Specialist Four with a grade of E-4. This rank is equivalent to a corporal. My pay was increased a little bit more and Yolanda and I started seriously thinking about moving to a larger place; that way when the baby came, we would have room to properly take care of her (We did not know at the time her sex. It was not as now when you know right away). We also received the good news that Yolanda's mother Maria Teresa (Tete) was coming to live with us to help after the birth. We found a one-bedroom apartment in the city of Columbia, South Carolina. It fit within our limited budget. Our good friends, the Puerto Rican couple that lived in the next trailer, also moved next to us at the new location.

The number of trainees signing up for the Catechism classes was increasing as the Army continued to draft more and more Puerto Ricans. These individuals were very young and many came from the interior of the island. These were very good people drafted into an untenable situation. These trainees did not speak English for the most part and were been used as "carne de cañon" (Cannon Fodder) in Vietnam. We were working hard and trying to keep up with an ever-increasing demand. Somehow we all want to get closer to God when we see ourselves in danger. It was very rewarding to see them come in scared and with a high degree of anxiety, and after the classes when they received the sacraments of Confession and Communion, seeing how they felt a lot better. Their smiling faces told us how grateful they were to God for this opportunity.

Every week for the coming months the number of trainees wanting religious instructions increased. We were concerned that we would reach a point when the quality of our classes would decrease due to the size of the classes and our limited time. Father Evangelisto and I met about this problem and decided that we needed another Spanish speaking assistant. This person would help to prepare this ever-increasing number of trainees needing religious instruction.

My friend Claudio Benedi, who at one time, like me, was waiting for orders to OCS, was now permanently assigned as a military policeman, called MPs. Claudio also made fun of me because I was a chaplain assistant and he was an MP. Exhibiting the Cuban trait of kidding around and making fun of our own shadows, he was always comparing the two jobs and saying that his was a much better job with more important responsibilities.

God works in mysterious ways, I am convinced. One day when I was driving the chaplain to a graduation parade out in the parade field, God provided for the assistant we needed. At the end of the event it started to rain really hard and as I was driving out of the field there was an MP standing in the rain directing traffic. Who was this "lucky" MP? None other than Claudio Benedi himself, soaking wet waving his hands and arms as if the rain was not happening. As I passed him, I rolled my window of the staff car down and said to him with a very sarcastic tone: "Goodbye MP!" Claudio looked at me and I could see in his face signs of frustration and maybe even anger. On my way back to the chapel, I thought of calling Claudio and offering him the possibility to be considered as our new chaplain assistant. I spoke to Father Evangelisto and he agreed to speak with him. I spoke to Claudio; and he was also in agreement. Later Claudio became our new chaplain assistant.

Claudio was and is a devout Catholic and knowledgeable in the many areas that were necessary to do his job. He was especially equipped to teach catechism to our trainees from Puerto Rico. There was only one problem, as Claudio expressed to me; he could not carry a tune. His singing ability was almost absent from his set of skills and all chaplain assistants were required to sing in order to lead the congregation during the Masses. I told him not to worry, that I would personally coach him. I also told him that for the most part the congregation would know the hymns and all he needed to do was to start with the first few words of the melody and then the congregation would do the rest. He then accepted the position. I served as his mentor and we went to his first Mass, not without practicing extensively the first sentence of every hymn that was assigned. Claudio was standing behind the lectern as Mass was ready to get started. He nervously announced: "The entrance hymn will be Holy, Holy, Holy. Please join me in the singing." He sang the first sentence and the congregation did not continue. This was probably the shortest entrance hymn in the history of Fort Jackson. He later became better at the singing and was very good at all the other duties.

The catechism classes continued quite well and many more were baptized and a lot more made their first confession and First Communion. Then something unpredictable happened. Father Evangelisto got orders to go to Vietnam as he had requested, and the Spanish Mass and the ability to hear confession in Spanish was leaving with him.

Chapter Twenty Four
The U.S. Army Part Eight:
God writes straight with
crooked lines

After Father Evangelisto left for Vietnam, none of the priests at Fort Jackson spoke Spanish, and as a result the 12:15 PM Mass at Chapel 10 could have been cancelled. This would have had a very negative effect in the community that attended it. It was the Mass with the largest congregation. The reasons for this Mass' popularity were three: there were many Spanish-speaking families at the fort; there were many trainees coming from Puerto Rico, as mentioned before; and father Evangelisto was a very charismatic preacher that was able to maintain the attention of the congregation and keep all of us coming back for more.

The Post Chaplain at the time was, Father Frain, a "full bird" Colonel (The bird refers to the Colonel insignia which is an eagle). He was an extremely experienced chaplain and a very devoted man, but his demeanor was stern and serious, not like Father Evangelisto. One day Father Frain called me into his office to ask my opinion of an idea that would give the Spanish Mass a chance to survive. Father Frain explained that because the priests had to learn Latin at the seminary, it would be relatively easy for them to read the Mass in Spanish given that many Spanish words derive from Latin. He needed my help in two ways. One, he wanted me to coach the different chaplains every week by reading with them the prayers and scriptures of that week, so that they would do a better job while reading them. I told him I had no problem with that. The second activity that he wanted me to do was one that gave me a lot of trepidation and feelings of unworthiness. Father Frain wanted me to give the sermon. "Now that is too much for me," I said. I felt that as a newly converted Catholic, I was not qualified to do it and I also felt that, a sinner like me, was not worthy of such a responsibility.

Father Frain quoted the famous Proverb: "God writes straight with crooked lines," explaining that even though he agreed that I was not fully prepared for that, I was the only one, at the time, who could do it, until another alternative was found. I asked him to give me a day to think, pray, and talk it over with Yolanda before I decided. He did not like that because in the Army you are supposed to follow orders, but he reluctantly agreed. I went home and Yolanda was as surprised as I was, but told me that she would help me and that made me feel better. Yolanda had, and still does have, a deep knowledge and faith that I did not have. The next day I told Father Frain that I would do it, but that we needed to find a permanent solution, not only for the Mass, but also for the confessions of the catechism students and others who did not speak English or prefer to do their confession in Spanish.

Yolanda and I began to prepare the first "sermon." I would write it and she would read it and make suggestions and corrections. Her training as a leader at Cursillos of Christianity and "rollista" was extremely helpful and I felt somewhat confident that I could do it. My training on the stage gave me some support to minimize the natural fear of speaking in public and Yolanda's support minimized the fear of preaching the wrong message. That Sunday came and my sermon was well received and the chaplain did his reading in Spanish quite well. We worked on the sermons for several weeks avoiding grave mistakes that could have precipitated my excommunication. Claudio Benedi also took turns with the sermon and that was a big help.

The other problem was the inability of the trainees to go to the Sacrament of Confession in English while meeting all the requirements for a good confession.

The requirements for a good confession are:

- Examination of Conscience
- Sorrow for having offended God
- A resolution of sinning no more
- Confession of our sins
- Satisfaction of penance

Our classes prepared them in a way that they could meet the first three requirements on their own before going to confession, but the last two were more challenging.

There were many who were ready for it, but could not do it. I came up with an "out-of-the-box" idea. This idea required training for both the trainees and the priests. All the trainees who were ready knew the Ten Commandments not only in content but also by their numbers. They also were given the names in English of the most common prayers used as penance. They knew the numbers in English, so they would go to confession "by-the-numbers." They would each say the number associated with the commandment against which they had sinned and then the number of times that they had done it. For example: Number 8 (You shall not bear false witness) 4 times or Number 6 (You shall not commit adultery) 2 times. After the absolution, the priest would tell them how many "Our Fathers" or "Hail Marys" they needed to pray as their penance and that was that. We were able to fulfill the last two require-ments. When I told Father Frain, he agreed.

There was an important part of the Sacrament that even though it is not required, is very helpful. That is the counsel-ing that the priest offers, from his training and experience of having heard many confession, as to what steps to take to pre-vent additional sins. That part they did not have. All I could do, if they asked me, was to give them my suggestion based on my own limited experience.

During those days a good friend, who was one of the mu-sicians in the band that I played in the show Añorada Cuba, Jose (Pepe) Pino, had also been drafted and was finishing his truck driver training in Fort Jackson when I came across him. He was also married and he joined our small group in a few social and sport activities. Pepe came to me one day because he was almost finished with his training and was very worried that he would be sent to Vietnam. He asked me if I could find out for him. I told him that this was not easy and practically impossible for me, but that I would ask around and see if any of the Cuban officers could help.

The first person I asked was Captain Candido Molinet, be-cause he had become a very good friend and he had a lot of contacts. He was always willing to help. He thought for a few seconds and told me that he would try. He was quite creative, resourceful, and fun to be around. I think he saw this situation as an opportunity to have fun and at the same time try to get the information about the upcoming orders for Pepe Pino. He asked me what was Pepe's company and also to meet him the next day at his home. He "ordered" me to dress in my class "A" uniform (Formal attire) and bring the chaplain's staff car. I did as he said and the next morning I was there.

We drove towards the personnel office and he told me to open the door of the car for him when we get there and to act as if he was a very important officer. He was dressed with all his medals and extremely shiny boots. He really looked like a very important officer. I opened the door for him and we both walked in the building. I was at his left, as it is required by Army protocol. The higher-ranking officer always walks in the extreme right and to his left the others also in ranking order. Several of the soldiers walking in the building saluted him, and he returned the salute with quickness and superb style. He was playing the part to the hilt. We got in front of the desk of the clerk who was in charge of Pepe's company's records. He asked the clerk for Jose Pino's personnel file. The clerk did not even question why. He was just so impressed with Molinet, that he just followed the order. In a few minutes the clerk brought the file. Molinet opened it and looked for the pending orders. He closed the file, gave it back to the clerk, did a perfect about-face and we both walked back to the staff car. I opened the door for him and got in the driver's seat to drive away. When I asked him what information he saw he said in typical Cuban expressive style: "Se jodió Pepe Pino." His orders were to Vietnam.

I called Pepe to tell him and he was very emotional because he had to leave his wife who was pregnant at the time. A few days passed and Pepe Pino's orders came in as told by Molinet. He was resigned to go when an unexpected event took place. Because French President Charles de Gaulle forced American troops out of France in 1966, the U.S. Support Operations Task Force Europe (SOTFE) needed to relocate its headquarters from Panzer Kaseme in France to

Stuttgart, Germany. Because of that, Pepe's orders were changed. The Army needed drivers to transport this base to Germany, and Pepe Pino was not sent to Vietnam and spent most of his time in Germany.

Chapter Twenty Five
The U.S. Army Part Nine:
Yolanda Maria was born

My wife Yolanda had a relatively easy pregnancy and she never exhibited those excessive stereotypical behaviors that women experience during these difficult months. One time when we were talking to my parents on the phone, Yolanda casually mentioned to my Dad that she longed to have a Cuban sandwich and my Dad sent one in the mail. Yolanda maintained her personality and attitude as nothing different was happening. We were both very nervous mainly because we did not know what to expect and at that time Yolanda went to several classes at the hospital and received some information, but there were no intensive classes as we now have. Yolanda would go to the monthly visit with the doctor at Fort Jackson Hospital and every time she was seen by a different doctor. In the Army at that time you could not select one doctor. That was somewhat uncomfortable, but we had no choice.

The original delivery date was estimated to be in the middle of November. When the middle of November arrived and nothing happened, we got even more nervous about the whole thing. Yolanda started to get really sensitive and every little move made by the baby, created concern. We did not have a phone; we could not afford one, and so every time there was some concern, I would go to the phone booth about two blocks away and call the hospital. The nurse who answered would then ask me questions and I would try to do the best I could to answer them. Some of these times, we were asked to come in for a checkup. We got in the car and drove to the hospital where they checked her and sent us back home at least three times with "false alarms." Most of these episodes occurred in the middle of the night and at very low temperatures.

The night of November 30, 1966 the contractions became stronger and when I called, the nurse again said to bring Yolanda in to be checked. This time Tete, my mother-in-law, came with us. When we arrived this very tall and heavyset nurse, who was a colonel, took her in and we waited in a small reception area where there were no chairs. It was around 11:00 PM. A few minutes later the stern nurse came out and in a very rude and insensitive manner told me that Yolanda was not quite ready, but that they were going to keep her this time. The nurse told me to go home and they would call me. I told her that we did not have a phone and asked her if we could stay there and wait. To which she replied no because it was against regulations. We needed to go somewhere that had a phone and we needed to give her that phone number.

I did not know what to do. Where could we go? What would happen if something went wrong and we could not be contacted? Was I going to miss the news of the baby's birth?

Then Tete came up with an idea. She remembered that our good friend, Gloria Fajardo, had told us to call her if we ever needed anything. Gloria, as mentioned before, was the wife of Captain Jose Fajardo, a Bay of Pigs hero and part of the Cuban cadre of officer stationed in Fort Jackson. We told the "nice' nurse that we would be back with the phone number in a few minutes and went to the nearest phone booth to call

Gloria. (Where were cellular phones back then when I needed them?) Gloria was most gracious and asked us to come to her house and spend the night while Yolanda was in labor, and that we could give the phone number to colonel "Nightingale."

Yolanda's experiences that night were really difficult. She was there by herself; she had never met any of the medical personnel before, the pain was very strong and worst of all, she did not know what was going on due to her lack of experience and information. Tete and I spent the entire night sitting in the Fajardos' living room next to the phone. To complicate matters even further, the next day I had a mandatory requalification for the M16 rifle. This event was going to take most of the morning and even though I requested to be excused, I could not get out of it. I went to the range while Tete stayed at Gloria's home. My thoughts were fixed on Yolanda and the baby and I could not care less about the requalification, the M16, the range, or the Army. I actually did it very nonchalantly and not really trying to do my best as I always try to do, but to my surprise I qualified as "expert."

I asked for the afternoon off and then I went to the Fajardos' and everything was the same. As we say in Cuba quoting the lyrics from a famous song of the early 30s: "El cuartico está igualito." (The little room has not changed). I called the hospital several times to get information, but was not given any more than "we will call you." Yolanda was going through hell and back not only with the pain, but also with the lack of information or my support. Yolanda had never seen the doctor who delivered the baby. Finally around 8:00 PM on December 1, 1966, we got a call that the birth was near and that we should come to the hospital. At around 9:00 PM Yolanda Maria was born and everything was fine. A few minutes later we were able to see the baby and visit with Yolanda who was exhausted and very glad to see familiar faces. Yolanda Maria was a beautiful baby and we were all very happy and thankful to God for His help throughout this event.

On December 18, 1966, Yolanda Maria Ochoa was baptized by Chaplain Father John Tobin at Fort Jackson's Chapel 10. The godparents were Ondina Menocal and Alex Casals who drove from Miami to South Carolina for the occasion. Coincidentally this date, December 18, was also my parents wedding anniversary. Yolanda's and my first wedding anniversary was only two days away on December 20. Later we had a small party at our apartment for a few of our friends. The group included Father Tobin. Mrs. Ross, Chapel 10's secretary and her husband, Claudio Benedi and his wife Mery, several Cuban officers and their families. Among the guests was a pretty little girl daughter of Captain and Gloria Fajardo by the name of Glorita. (This pretty little girl was to become a world-renowned entertainer known as Gloria Estefan). We took some pictures, and I used our newly acquired 8 millimeter movie camera for the first time.

In January my parents and my sister Susy came from Miami to visit us and meet what was my father's first grandchild. It was pretty cold those days in Columbia, South Carolina. I believe it was in the low 20s. My family was not used to this weather, and their trip by car had been very difficult and long. That Sunday the visitors came to Mass with us at Chapel 10 and were very surprised to see that I was giving the sermon. My parents' faces when I started the sermon had a mixed expression between amazement and disbelief.

My parents were so happy to see Yoli-Mari, as we started to call her. She was a beautiful baby. As any baby, (we know this now, but not then) was crying a lot and we decided, foolishly, that we would not pick her up every time she cried so we could "train" her to be a "good" baby. That did not sit well with my mother, who would pick up Yoli-Mari anytime she started crying. I then made one of the most regretful mistakes of my life. I told my mother not to pick Yoli-Mari up. My mother insisted and told me that I was wrong and that she knew what to do. In my nervousness and lack of experience, I refuted my mother's suggestion and told her in a very stupid way that; "This is my daughter and I can raise her as I see fit." My mother then told me that she had raised 4 children and that she knew more than I did. I then said: "You did it your way and I will do it mine." This unfortunate dialogue provoked my parents, my sister, and her husband, to leave immediately and I felt like an idiot. I later apologized to my mother, but what I said hurt her. She forgave me.

There is a very delicate balance between the genuine help from grandparents, when we have children, and interference. That incident set the tone for my relationship with my parents in reference to our children and even though I made a terrible mistake in how I voiced my opinion, it helped draw some boundaries for the future. I also learned how to act as a grandparent when my children had their own children. Now that we have our own grandchildren, Yolanda and I are there when they need us, but we do not assume the full responsibility. The responsibility rests on the parents. If we are asked for advice, we gladly offer some. If we see that they are doing something that could be done better, in our view, we are very careful with unsolicited, albeit well-meaning advice.

Chapter Twenty Six
The U.S. Army Part Ten:
Military life minus War, not so bad!

L ife in the army, now that I was not going to be sent to Vietnam, was not so bad. The tour of duty in Viet-Nam was for a minimum of thirteen months and I was already "too short." My job as chaplain's assistant was difficult because of the number of hours that were required, but I was doing something that I liked and at the same time I felt good helping my fellow soldiers.

Claudio Benedi and I continued to take turns preaching the Sunday sermons, but both felt that we were not really prepared for it. Taking advantage that Claudio's father, Claudio Benedi Sr. was visiting his son, we asked him to preach for us that Sunday. Claudio Sr. was an attorney and also a very devout Catholic. He was a recognized speaker and often offered dissertations in Washington DC where he was well connected. He was a member of the blossoming Cuban-American leadership. Claudio Sr. was a true speaker and gave an outstanding sermon.

I felt that a permanent solution to the lack of a Spanish speaking priest was necessary, so I spoke to Father Frain, who felt the same way, about an idea that I had. I would find a Spanish speaking priest in Miami, where I had many friends, so he could fly to Columbia for the weekend. The army would pay for the plane ticket, accommodations, and a fee for service. The priest would fly on Saturday morning, hear confessions Saturday afternoon, and would celebrate the Spanish Mass Sunday afternoon after which he would fly back to Miami. I would take care of the ground transportation and meals, and the army would do the rest. Father Frain liked the idea and asked me to search for such a willing priest.

Yolanda and I knew a number of priests in Miami and we went through the mental list until we came to Father Avelino Gonzalez. Father Avelino was Spanish from the Dominican order who worked out of Saint Dominic parish in northwest Miami and had worked with us in Cursillos. He would be ideal because he was semi-retired and did not have many duties at the parish. He was a gentle and loveable priest with a big heart and a soul full of the Holy Spirit. We both agreed that he was the best candidate. We called him and he agreed to the challenge. The logistics of the "mission" were as follows:

The office of the Post Chaplain would purchase the round trip plane tickets. Saturday: Miami-Columbia and Sunday Columbia-Miami.

My father, who was always willing to help us, would pick up Father Avelino on Saturday and take him to the airport.

Father Avelino would arrive at Columbia, S.C. airport where I would pick him up and take him to my home for lunch.

I would drive him to Chapel 10 for confessions and at the end take him to a local Catholic parish where they would give him dinner and a place to sleep. This was arranged by the Post Chaplain's office.

On Sunday I would pick him up and take him to Chapel 10 for the Spanish Mass. He would hear confession before the Mass as well.

After the Mass I would take him to lunch and later back to the airport

My father would pick him up at the airport and take him to his parish.

This "mission" worked well for several months and Father Avelino was a blessing to all of us, especially the congregation and in particular to the soldiers.

Living with just army pay was hard and we were always looking to make extra income. My mother-in-law, Tete, got a job at a local factory. I gave guitar lessons to several children of our friends in the Fort. Tete, Yolanda, and I took over the washing and ironing of all the linen used in Chapel 10. Yolanda was soon pregnant again with our second child who was due that December. We obviously needed to save some money because the child was going to be born two months after I had finished the army. That meant we did not have insurance to cover the cost of the doctor and the hospital. My mother-in-law, who had a great sense of humor used to say that "le sacamos el aceite a la aceituna" which means that we would squeeze the oil out of the olives. Meaning that we would take advantage of every minute of our time to work and produce.

One of my guitar students was a beautiful little girl about 9 years old named Glorita. She was the daughter of Jose and Gloria Fajardo. It was in their home that Tete and I stayed the night when our first daughter was born. After my first class, I told her mother Gloria that in my opinion Glorita had a great talent for music and that she learned very quickly. She was singing in perfect tune the children's songs that I was trying to teach her. Her timing was almost perfect too. Glorita had a natural talent for music, singing, and playing the guitar. In top of that she acted as she really enjoyed it. We now know this little girl as Gloria Estefan who is among the top musical stars of the world and the pride of the Cuban-American community. I am ever so honored and grateful to have, in a very small way, started her in the path that both Gloria and Emilio, her husband, have taken. They both continue to climb and remain at the top of their profession. I am proud to call them friends.

Because Cuban food products where non-existent in Columbia, South Carolina at the time, the small group of Cubans were always longing for black beans, guava paste, Cuban crackers, Cuban coffee, and more. I had become pretty good at coming up with ideas and planning logistics to positively influence our life. These ideas that combine benefits to all involved with no negative effects are the best. One of these ideas was to combine the apparent need of those Cubans in Columbia, S.C. for Cuban food; our family needs to earn extra income and Father Avellino's trips to help the soldiers.

I asked my father to temporarily finance the idea, given that we did not have any capital. He would buy different Cuban products, as much as could fit in a medium sized box. He would include a list of how much each item cost. Father Avelino would bring the box as his luggage at no charge, and I would sell it to the Cubans in Columbia, S.C. I would mark up the price given that the "supply" was low and the "demand" was high. This was a win-win situation and no one was hurt by it. The Cubans would get the products at a reasonable price, we would make some profit and send the rest to my father who was willing to wait to get paid, and Father Avelino was unaffected as well as the airline, given that Father Avelino did not have any other luggage.

The first "shipment" came in, and we then contacted the Cubans who at first were very happy to pay the extra price. Many of them made me special orders for the following week.

We did this for several weeks, but stopped when the demand dried up due to two things:

The longing for Cuban food was temporarily satisfied

My "customers" started to say that the prices were too high.

It was good while it lasted. I sent my father his "capital" back, and we made a little bit of money for our upcoming baby.

Chapter Twenty Seven
The U.S. Army Part Eleven:
The last few months

The last few months in the army continued to be enjoyable with the exception of one incident. Out of the blue, I receive orders to go to OCS (Officer Candidate School). It was a scary surprise because I had resigned OCS almost one year before and I only had a few months to go until the end of my two-year draft. If I were to be ordered to go to OCS, that would have extended my two years to more than five, and there was almost a 100% possibility that I would be sent to the war.

I took the orders and I went to the personnel office to find out why. The clerk that was there told me that it was an error and that I did not have to go. I asked him for something in writing and he denied my request. I left there somewhat more relieved, but not with a complete assurance that I was in the clear. I consulted with my superiors, and they all said that I did not have to worry. Easier said than done!

During those days I received a promotion to Specialist-5 (E-5). This rank is equivalent to sergeant. That meant a lot to me because I would get paid a little more, and also if you were separated (army talk for finishing) with this rank, the Army would pay for all my moving expenses. My promotion was due to all the work that I had done with the religious instruction classes, and the success of my plan for the Spanish

Mass. For the same reasons, I later received the highest commendation medal given for non-war related merits: The Army Commendation Medal. I was very proud of that, and I shared it with Yolanda, my wife, who helped me so much with the classes.

Several of my fellow soldiers, whose time was also running short in the Army were called to the recruiting office to be given a pep talk and to try to entice them to re-enlist. I was also called after talking to my first sergeant, my company executive officer, and my company commander. All three tried in vain to make me re-enlist. I went to my appointment with the recruiting Master Sergeant, who offered me all kinds of perks and money to do it. He offered me a cash re-enlistment bonus and to be sent to OCS. I did not want to re-enlist, go to OCS or go to war. I had heard that the Army recruiter would call you several times to try to convince you.

My wife, Yolanda, was expecting our second child who was going to be born in December after my separation in October, so I asked the recruiting sergeant if I could re-enlist for 6 months. He told me that the shortest time was 3 years. Trying to eliminate any subsequent visits to the recruiting office, I then told him that I would re-enlist. His face lit up thinking he had convinced me, but then I said: "I would re-enlist for how many months you want, but only under one condition that I needed in writing, and approved by the Post Commander. He asked: What condition is that? Then I said: "The condition is that I would be sent to Cuba to fight Castro as a U.S army soldier within six months." The sergeant told me that he could not do that. I told him: "When you can, call me back."

The strategy worked because I was never called back. I guess they figured I was either crazy or a ferocious Cuban patriot. I was neither. I just wanted out of the Army, and I did not want to be called again and again for a pep talk.

October 25, 1967, came and I was discharged honorably from the U.S. Army. Uncle Sam paid the entire move back to Hialeah, and the four of us drove back in our 1965 Plymouth Valiant. I was happy with my accomplishments in the army, for what I had learned, and with a tremendous satisfaction to have served the United States military. I have grown as a person, as a husband, as a father and as a Christian. All of these would come very handy in the years to come.

Chapter Twenty Eight
Back to South Florida
for the "last" time

As the plane was approaching Miami International Airport on my way back, from my trip to San Diego, California, I remembered the time that our new family was approaching Miami after driving for a couple of days on the trip back from the U.S. Army and South Carolina. I remember thinking then what would be in store for us as we start again a new phase of our lives. When the plane touched down all those feelings of anxiety and fear came back to me. The difference was that now I not only had to take care of myself, but I had to provide for my wife and child, as well as the child that was arriving very soon.

My parents and my sister Susy where living in Puerto Rico at the time. Because of that, there was room for us on a temporary basis in the house that my parents and my sister, Cecilia were renting in Hialeah. My sister Cecilia lived there with her husband, Ruben, her son Rubencito, her daughter, Cecilia, and my grandmother Coloma. Yolanda, Tete, the baby, and I moved into my old room. We were very crowded and almost immediately started to look for an apartment to rent. Yolanda was on her seventh month of her second pregnancy, and we needed room for the new baby scheduled for late December 1967.

I went back to my old job selling used cars at Deel Ford in Coral Gables. They were happy to see me back. A lot had changed in my life since I left this job in October 1965, when I was single and living at home without any financial obligations. I did not have a daughter, had not gone through the experiences of the Army, and was a lot more mature. Selling, and especially selling used cars, is not an easy job. Before the Army, I did not have the pressure to sell. Whatever I sold, was "sufficient." My relaxed attitude then, helped me be more effective, and I did not need to apply some of the deceptive tactics that my counterparts applied on a normal basis to accomplish high levels of sales.

Things were now different for me. I was only given $75.00 per week as an advance against future commissions, and that was not enough to make ends meet, so I had the pressure to sell at a much higher level than before. I did not want to utilize the previously mentioned questionable tactics, so my sales were not enough, and many weeks I did not earn sufficient commission to cover the advance. The deficiency was accumulated and I was getting really stressed out about it. The manager was very understanding and called me to his office several times to try to help me out and to tell me that I needed to perform better. My fellow salesmen also tried to help me, but my mind and attitude was not the same as before. I was really struggling.

My wife was about to have the baby, we did not have medical insurance, we needed to find an apartment, and I needed to make more money and find a "regular" job. It was not easy to find a job given my lack of formal education. Viet-Nam veterans were sometimes looked at in a negative light due to all the bad press that the war received from the news media. I looked in the newspaper every day for opportunities and there were not very many for my qualifications, or lack thereof.

One day the newspaper ad read: "No experience necessary. We train you to be an assistant manager. We offer salary plus bonuses. Call (the phone number) Tom Thumb Stores." This caught my attention because this was a convenience store where my prior experience in the grocery business could come in handy. So I applied and got the job in their store in Hialeah at Okeechobee Road near Palm Avenue. I was trained for three weeks and then I was given to "manage" the third shift. My schedule was from 11:30 PM to 7:30 AM, and I was the only person in the store. It is really easy to be a manager when you only have to deal with yourself. After a few weeks I got the hang of the job, but the hours were killing me.

Tete, my mother-in-law, found a small two-bedroom apartment in Hialeah, near the racetrack and we moved in. On December 27, 1967 our beautiful baby girl Maria Teresa Ochoa was born at Baptist Hospital in Kendall. We called her Mari Teri. The cost of the doctor and the hospital pretty much consumed our small savings, but we were not worried because I now had a fairly steady job and maybe a future with the company. Our total adjusted income for 1967, which included the Army, Deel Ford, and Tom Thumb was a whopping $3,168. This income would be $22,176 in 2014 dollars after an average inflation rate of 4.13%. Imagine how someone supporting a family of 4 with this income and no additional federal or state assistance could survive. Well we did it.

Mari Teri was baptized at the Immaculate Conception parish in Hialeah by Father Miguel, the priest who married us. The godparents were my sister, Pepita, and her husband Vicente (Pupy) Calle. My grandmother, Coloma, was there, my sister Cecilia and her family, as well as a few friends. The ceremony was full of emotions for me due to the presence of Father Miguel, its location, the parish where I took my first steps after my conversion in Cursillos, the absence of my parents, and the uncertainty of my future.

One evening when I was working at Tom Thumb, my good friend from Añorada Cuba, Luis (Wichy) Puga, came into the store and he was surprised to see me there. We talked for a while to catch up with our lives. I was happy to see him. Wichy was the conga player for our band and he was very good at it. We had become good friends those days. He told me he was working for Winn Dixie stores as a manager at the meat department at the store located in SW 8 street and 23 Avenue in Miami. He asked me how much I was making and when I told him, he said that I could make a lot more at Winn Dixie with a lot better hours. He offered to recommend me to the store manager for a position as stock clerk in the groceries department. I told him that would be great. A few days later I went to see the store manager at Winn Dixie.

It was early 1968 and I met with Bill Trujillo, the store manager. Mr. Trujillo was from Cuba, but he was not a political refugee. He migrated to the U.S. before 1959 and spoke both very good English and Spanish. We had a good interview and he offered me the job of stock clerk for a few more dollars a week, but a lot better schedule. Winn Dixie also offered excellent benefits and opportunities for advancement. Because of all my prior experience I was assigned to stock several sections of the store, plus cashiering when necessary. During those days we found out that Yolanda was pregnant again with our third child.

We soon found a larger apartment in the North West section of Miami nearer my job. This was an up-and-down duplex near the Miami River. The lady, owner of the duplex, lived on the bottom floor, and we lived on the top one. The rent was a little higher, but it had two bedrooms and another room, called Florida room, which was converted into a bedroom for Tete. We only had one bathroom, but we made do. Tete started to work in an electronics factory and contributed to the family not only financially, but especially with her support and her presence. Tete was the ideal mother-in-law.

Chapter Twenty Nine
Winn Dixie's robbery

My job at Winn Dixie was progressing well and even though Trujillo was hard to get along with, my training in discipline and endurance in the Army helped me deal with him, and he was pleased with me. The work was physical and repetitious, but I was good at it. One of our jobs was to strip down the floor of our sections, mop them clean, and re-wax them every 3 months. Even at this very low level task, I took pride when Trujillo told me that my sections' floors looked the best. Another task was to unload the weekly truck that brought in the groceries to replenish our inventory. This task took place in the backroom of the store with no air conditioning. A crew of three men was assigned to this task. One would be at the back of the trailer truck and would place each box into a metal roller-conveyor. The other two would lift the boxes from the conveyor and place them on the shelves that were organized according to the layout of the store. This exercise did me good, and I did not have to go to the gym and pay money that I did not have, to stay in shape.

One of my duties was to be there every morning at 8:00 AM, bring in the stack of fresh bread boxes left outside the store, and place all the bread on the shelves at the back of the store, after removing those pieces that had expired dates. One morning while I was doing this task, I saw the Doctor Pepper truck driver, who used to come every morning to deliver new product, coming toward me as he did every morning, but this time he had a young black man at his side. I thought that finally this older man was getting some help. I was very wrong. As they approach me I said to them: "Good morning!" as I did every day. I see then that the young black man had a gun in his hand and ran toward me hitting me with the barrel of the gun on the left side of my head as he was saying: "Good morning son of a bitch." As I fell to the ground from the blow, semi-unconsciously I heard him say: "Get up you son of a bitch or I blow your brains out," while placing the 38 caliber revolver on the side of my forehead. I got up really fast and then began to feel the blood from the head wound dripping down my neck. He took me and the Doctor Pepper driver to the backroom, told us to lie down on the floor. He kicked us all over our bodies and then proceeded to take our wallets. He then left and told us not to move for a while. It seemed like an eternity not knowing how bad my wound was.

While this was going on with us in the back of the store, there were two other robbers trying to get the money from the vault. They also hit Trujillo before he opened the vault. They took the money and left. When I felt it was safe, I got up and stumbled to the front of the store. When Trujillo saw me and my bloody white shirt, he called the ambulance. I was transported to Jackson Memorial Hospital's emergency room where I got eight stitches on my head. I had not called Yolanda at this point because I did not want to scare her without her seeing that I was okay. She was pregnant and I did not want to risk it. One of my coworkers picked me up at the hospital and brought me back to the store to pick up my car. I then drove home and when Yolanda saw me she was visible very upset, but I told her I was okay and then told her the story. I changed shirts, took two aspirins, and went back to work. I could not afford to miss my hours.

When I got back to the store I found out the whole story. The automatic "out" door of the store was opened and when the different delivery guys would come in, someone from the inside would step on the doormat, the door would open, and they would come in. One of those times, the robbers also came in. Since that time the procedure was changed and the delivery guys had to come in through the front door that would have to be unlocked every time. I continued my work as if nothing had happened. Trujillo did not send me home, he did not give light duty, and he acted as if nothing had happened. He was a task oriented manager and not to concerned with people and his relationship with them.

Several weeks later as I was covering as cashier, a "shopper" came in and shopped me. Shoppers in this context refer to "fake" customers, paid by the company to visit the stores and then prepare a report with the results of the visit. My report was mostly acceptable except, according to this shopper, I did not say "good morning" to him. When the report was received, Trujillo called me to his office. The district manager was also there and both proceeded to reprimand me for my lack of customer service skills. I listened to them calmly and when they finished I told them: "You take the time to talk to me after the results of this shop and you reprimand me because I did not said good morning. You have forgotten that because I said good morning to the robber a few days back, I was hit on the head, had eight stitches on my head, and neither Trujillo, nor you Mr. District Manager (I do not remember his name) came to talk to me and did not even ask me how I felt, and allowed me to work the day of the injury. I should have sued you, as many friends told me to do, but I did not. This is how I get paid for my loyalty and hard work." I asked them if they were finished and I went back to work. Trujillo did not change his attitude, but the district manager made a point every time he came to the store to seek me out and ask me how I was doing.

Chapter Thirty
Following my wife's advice and my first son was born

"Wives can be anchors that stop your
journey or sails that facilitate it"
Author Unknown

As mentioned before, while I was working at Winn Dixie, my wife got pregnant with our third child and our economic situation was very weak. At Winn Dixie I took every opportunity to work overtime. I even worked every Sunday as the Sunday manager and I got paid double-time. I had another job with a company called Polanco Inc., which distributed Spanish food to Non-Hispanic supermarkets, and I was also giving guitar lessons. My really good friend, Manolo Toyos, got me the job with Polanco. Manolo passed away already, but he was a great friend and a very devout Catholic. The Polanco's job consisted of going to these grocery stores and replenishing their Spanish Foods' section. I would then order for the following week when I would stock the section again. It was a great job for me because I could do it at any time and did not interfere with my full time job at Winn Dixie. All these efforts barely made our "ends meet" at the end of the month. The coming of our third child would add to our expenses, and Yolanda and I had several talks about our alternatives.

In one of those conversations Yolanda suggested that I needed to go back to school, get more education or training, so I could then aspire to get a better paying job. She had already done her homework and recommended that I study computer programming, which at the time was an up-and-coming career as our society was beginning to see the advantages of computers. I knew that I did not like school. My previous experience with school had left me with low self-confidence in my abilities to succeed in school. I also told her that we did not have any additional funds that could be used to pay for the school, but she also had a plan for that: The GI Bill would pay for the school up to 36 months. One and one half months for every month I served in the Army. Yolanda had even found a school that was nearby. The school was called: Florida Computer College in downtown Miami near the Brickell Bridge.

I went to the school and took their entrance exam and passed it with flying colors and was accepted. I spoke to Trujillo, Winn Dixie's manager, to see if I could arrange my schedule to attend school in the morning and work in the afternoons, evenings, and weekends. Trujillo was hesitant and tried to talk me out of it saying that my future was with Winn Dixie, but eventually agreed to do it. He knew that I was a good worker who got things done "his" way and he did not want to lose me. Cuban entrepreneurs owned Florida Computer College, and most of the instructors were Cubans. The classes were in English and most of the students were young Cubans like me. One of the owners and professor of programming was Jorge Utset, who has become one of my best friends. Jorge Utset was a wonderful professor, and he was very well versed in the programming languages used at the time. Today Jorge Utset runs one of the best websites with true information about what is really happening in Cuba. It is: www.therealcuba.com

During the time I was in school, my first son, Rolando Marcos Ochoa was born on February 8, 1969 at Baptist Hospital in Kendall. After having two girls, I was almost sure that this one would be a girl too. I really loved my daughters and they are wonderful, but I wanted to have a son in order to, among other things, pass my last name to the next generation. Back then the fathers were not allowed in the delivery room as they are a now, so I sat in the Baptist Hospital's maternity waiting area for a long time. After about two hours or so, I went to the nurses' desk and asked if they had any news. She told me that my son was born about one hour ago, and she was surprised that the doctor did not come out to tell me. I was really upset and when the doctor came to talk to me I told him so. He apologized and took me to see Yolanda and the baby.

He was beautiful and we were very happy everything was alright with both mother and baby. Fortunately, we had medical insurance through Winn Dixie, which covered most of the costs. In a few days she went home to our small apartment in the northwest section of Miami. Shortly thereafter, "Rolin," as we called him, was baptized at Saint Michael's Catholic Church in Miami by none other than Father Miguel. His godparents were Terina, Yolanda's cousin and her husband Rene Smith.

We only had one car. The same car we had while I was in the army, so I needed additional transportation, but we did not have the money for another car. I went to Sears near Coral Gables' Miracle Mile and bought a Moped for about $70.00 on credit. This would solve the transportation problem and would not increase our gas consumption by much. Also parking in downtown Miami was expensive and scarce, so the moped could be parked anywhere at no cost.

The course at Florida Computer College consisted of programming, system analysis and accounting and was for 10 months after which the school would help you find a job. I met a lot of good people at the school, both professors and students, and made some real good friendships. Most of my fellow students were also young recently married men who were struggling with work and school and little money to even have lunch in the area. I thought of an idea to help me get more money and at the same time help my classmates. I told the idea to my mother-in-law, and then Tete and I started a lunch delivery "business." I would take the order for the following day and then Tete would prepare the sandwiches and I would deliver them the next day. Tete and I split the small profit, but every little thing helped us to meet our ever-increasing expenses.

I successfully completed the course in May 1969 and got very high grades to my surprise. I felt that I was a proficient programmer and ready to tackle one of the many jobs that were available at the time. Given my good record, I got a job at a company called Crane Cams located in Hallandale Florida, as a computer operator. At the time most people started as operators and then worked their way up to programming. They were paying me less than at Winn Dixie, but I needed to "pay my dues." Trujillo, Winn Dixie's manager, was very unhappy with my decision and tried hard to talk me out of it. I was determined to start this new profession and I did not change my mind. I resigned and gave them my two-week notice.

The first week Trujillo started to treat me even harder than before and showed his anger toward me by assigning me the harder jobs. One morning I came in and he asked me to clean the attic of the store. I was in that store for over four years and we had never cleaned that attic. This was obviously Trujillo's way of punishing me for leaving the company and him. I was very upset, but went ahead and cleaned the attic as told. On my break I called my new employer and asked them if I could start earlier and they said I could start at any time. I told them I would be starting the next day. After washing off all the dirt and sweat, I put my shirt back on and marched into Trujillo's office. I told him I was leaving effective immediately and that I was rescinding my notice. When he asked me why, I told him that I was not going to let him abuse me because I was leaving. I placed my keys and other equipment on his desk and walked out. As I was leaving he told me: Let me know if you want a part-time job in the future. I did not answer him.

We needed to buy a bigger car in order to fit all three kids, so we bought a 1969 Volkswagen bus. It was light blue and had a side door, very convenient to get the kids in and out of it. This vehicle was the first minivan in the market. It was stick shift, but Yolanda already knew how to drive it. I really liked this vehicle, and we had a lot of fun with it. As many of you know, this vehicle became the favorite of many "hippies," but also was perfect for families with a lot of kids. My good friend Manolito Campa and his wife Carmen, who had 5 children, also had the same vehicle, but a different color. We would drive together to the Keys or Crandon Park, and when we got there people probably thought we were on a school outing. Life was simple, but full of joy and happiness.

I only worked at Crane Cams for a few months, because the owner of Florida Computer College called and asked me to join a new company they had formed. They had created what was called a service bureau. These were companies that were contracted by other companies that wanted to outsource their programming and computer operation service and not do it in-house. The company was called Data Applications and was a subsidiary of Florida Computer College. I started at Data Applications as a programmer/operator. Our main customer was Florida Computer College and we did all their accounting, payroll, and student records applications. I helped program some of these applications, and I was the main operator who ran them. We had other clients as well.

After a few months at Data Applications, I was told that the business was closing and I was given a month to find another job. I started to apply all over the place, but could not get any offers. My problem was simple and at the same time difficult. I did not have enough experience as a programmer and the companies did not want to hire me as an operator because they feared that the moment I would find a programming job, I would quit. So on one hand I had too little experience and on the other I had too much. It was really frustrating as the end of the 30 days drew near. I saw myself back at Winn-Dixie.

Chapter Thirty One
How did I became a banker?

I had filled out several dozen employment applications and none of them resulted in a job offer. I had about 15 days to go at Data Applications when my Dad and Mom told me about this couple they had met at an event they participated in. The man was a banker and had an important job at a bank in Fort Lauderdale, and he told my parents for me to call him for a job. He was in charge of the computers at that bank. I thanked my parents and told them that I was going to call him even though I thought that a bank would never hire me given my lack of college education and limited programming experience.

I continued my job search and filled out many more applications for employment, but nothing seemed to produce a job. Now I was not only worried, but also desperate because I had just a few days left, and after that I would not have any income. Our savings were minimal due to all our expenses and my low salary. One day I remembered the banker that had offered help, and I decided to call him and see. What could happen? That he would say no? No, is all I had at that point.

I called Mr. Frank Menendez, Vice President and Cashier of First National Bank of Fort Lauderdale and made an appointment to meet him to see if he could help me. Menendez was an avid admirer of my family and was extremely friendly and nice during our meeting. He told me he was looking for someone like me because he wanted to promote the current supervisor of the Computer Operations Department and replace him with someone with my background and strong work-ethics. I found this scenario very surprising given my background. I had never been a supervisor, I did not know anything about banking, and I especially did not know anything about bank computer operations. He further explained that the current supervisor was an excellent banker but he did not want to be promoted. The supervisor's excuse, according to Menendez, was that he could not find any suitable candidate to replace himself. Menendez, his supervisor, wanted him to work during the day and supervise all three shifts plus other duties which would enlarge his job.

Menendez told me that I would be hired as an operator on the second shift and as I learned the processes, I would then be promoted to Manager of Night Operations. This sounded at the time like a corporate intrigue, but I needed a job and the pay was good, even if I had to drive for almost an hour one way, and work from 3 PM to 11 PM Monday through Friday. I decided to accept the job and thought that things would be sorted out once I started and even if I did not get the manager's job, my pay and benefits were excellent for May 1970. Also, because I would be working the second shift, I could work a part-time job during the morning hours if needed.

I reported to work and my supervisor was Manuel Fernandez-Grande, who was the manager of computer operations. Manuel and I hit it off fairly well from the beginning. He was a wonderful man, with a great sense of humor, and very charismatic leadership style. His subordinates loved him and the work environment was excellent. This bank functioned as a service bureau for other banks that outsourced their computer operation to it. At the time we were running all the computer work for about 50 banks in the tri-county area of South Florida. First National Bank of Fort Lauderdale was, at the time, the number one bank in South Florida, when it came to computer operation activities and the largest bank in Broward County. The bank was located in downtown Fort Lauderdale in the building where Broward College is now located on Las Olas Boulevard. The computer room occupied the entire 4th floor where two separate IBM 360s were installed with many disc drives and tape drives. Each of the computers had a check sorter installed where the paper checks were sorted and converted to electronic data. Just a desktop computer, thanks to the technological advances and the innovative mentality of humans, could now obtain the computing capacity of all this equipment.

My first job was sorter operator. This job consisted in running through the sorter drawers of deposited items (checks, deposit slips, savings items, etc) from all 50 banks. The sorter would then divide the deposited items into the different pockets and at the same time converts these paper items into electronic data. This data was later posted by the third shift to the customers' accounts. Each run of the sorter was then balanced by the balancing department including any rejects. After each bank was balanced, the items were then sorted by account numbers in a process called "fine sorting." The sorted items were then sent back to each bank for manual filing into the customers' files. These items would then be returned to the customers with their monthly statements. This may sound like ancient history to many today, given all the advances in electronic banking imaging.

The job was good, but not great, given its monotony and dependence on the sorters, which at times became jammed and broken. Paper checks and deposits have a lot of dust on them, so at the beginning, the dust made me sick and gave me a rash on my hands. After a few months as a sorter operator, I was transferred to the balancing department to continue my training. After a few months there I was promoted to Manager of Night Operations, and I had over 50 people reporting to me. This job was many sizes too big for me, but I accepted the challenge. I encountered a lot of passive resistance, but after a few weeks, I felt that a lot of the staff had accepted me. It was hard to replace Manuel because he so well liked, but I used some of his tactics, and I got close to the staff and tried to be a source for them. I was still a non-exempt (paid overtime) employee, so I was getting a lot of overtime. Sometimes my overtime pay was more than my regular pay.

All this while, I was working part time at none other than Winn Dixie for none other than Trujillo. He gave me some mornings and both Saturday and Sunday hours. Sunday hours were great, because I got paid double time, plus I acted as the manager. I was getting very little sleep, but I was able to make ends meet. During this time our fourth child, William Manuel Ochoa was born in Baptist Hospital on June 1, 1970. Willie, as we called him, was very handsome. Shortly thereafter he was baptized by Father Miguel at Saint Michael's Church in Miami. His godparents were my sister Cecilia and her husband Ruben Tamayo.

I also registered, after I got promoted, at Broward Community College to start taking morning classes. I was planning to stop working at Winn Dixie during the week, but continued to work on the weekend. The bank would pay for my classes and books, as long as I passed. Things were looking up for me and my family. Yolanda was a true champion taking care of all four children, who were only approximately one year apart. She is an excellent "domestic engineer" and worked very hard 24/7 for her family. When Willie was able to eat regular food, she used to sit all the other three in their highchairs around the dining room table, placed Willie in his infant seat in the middle of the table, and then proceeded to spoon feed all four in the same sitting. Everyone ate the same food, and by the time the first one fed finished swallowing, he or she was ready for the next spoonful. It was sort of a modified Henry Ford-assembly line. Tete, Yolanda's mother, was also very helpful and cooperated with us in everything.

Around that time Yolanda's sister, Ondina, lost her husband Ricardo Garcia Menocal. They were living in Atlanta Georgia. Given that Ondina was now by herself and her daughter Ondinita was living in New Jersey where it was too cold for Ondina, she came to live with us. Ondina took charge of Willie and helped Yolanda immensely. She also started to work as a seamstress and we had several salaries coming into the house. The negative side was that we only had one bathroom and three rooms for four adults and four children. It was hard for me to sleep during the day, but we managed and were very happy.

Chapter Thirty Two
The Only Constant Thing in Life
is Change.

The week before I was to start in Broward Community College, there was a shake up at the bank. Frank Menendez was no longer in charge of the computer operations and I was told that I was to be demoted to clerk in the balancing department on the first shift. I guessed that because I had been Menendez's protégé, I was also hurt by the changes. Menendez called me and told me not to worry that he was going to create a job in the Cashier's Department (Bank Operations and Accounting) for me. He also said that he would need some time, but it was a sure thing. I swallowed my pride, dropped my classes at Broward Community College, and reported to the balancing department as a clerk working from 9 to 5 with the same salary, but without overtime. I asked Trujillo to give me hours in the evening and was still doing the weekends.

My work ethic continued to show to all around me that I was a hard worker and that this change was not going to make me fail at anything. I had the feeling that some of the people in charge wanted me to quit, but I proved them wrong. I was the best balancer they had, because I knew how the night shift worked and knew were to go for information when things were out of balance. After a few months, as promised by Menendez, I was transferred to the Cashier's Department to a newly created position called: "Accounting Analyst." That sounded impressive, but I had very little knowledge of accounting and none as an analyst in the banking industry. Menendez knew that, but he told me he would teach me and he became my teacher and mentor.

Frank Menendez was a very good boss. He loved to train and share his vast knowledge of banking and accounting. He designed my job to be a liaison between the operating departments of the bank and the computer systems. I had some knowledge of the bank's computer system, but very little as to how a bank operated. He would send me to different departments that were having issues with the computer systems and my job was to analyze the problem and come up with solutions. I really enjoyed it and that gave me, very fast, a knowledge in a lot of areas that otherwise would have taken me many years to acquire. Menendez loved to assign projects to me and it seemed that every day he would come up with something else to analyze and resolve. Soon my "to-do-pile" was very tall and growing and growing.

There were not enough hours in a day to catch up. I decided to make a list of all the projects and go to Menendez and asked him to prioritize them, so I could complete those projects that he considered more important first and then the others. He was surprised to see the extent of the list and then assigned numerical priority to all of them. That made me feel a little better and I started to do them in the order he gave me. Once in a while he would give me another project and right away I would ask him to give me its priority. I found that this way I was doing what he wanted, and he was aware of the volume.

Working in the bank had made our finances a little better. By 1971, my first full year at First National Bank of Fort

Lauderdale, I made around $11,250 per year. In order to have the same purchasing power today (2015), I would need to make around $65,700 adjusted for inflation. We were not saving any money at the time, and the small rental apartment in Miami was getting smaller and smaller as the children started to grow. One day Menendez ask me tedo go to his office because he needed to tell me something important. I was anxious and asked myself why. Did I do something wrong? Why is it, that most of us when the boss calls us to his or her office, we think that something is wrong? Menendez asked me to close the door and to sit down. He explained that he was buying a new home in east Fort Lauderdale and that he was selling his house in Plantation. He proceeded to recommend that I buy his house; because he knew that we were not comfortable in our apartment and also that I would be very close to work and save on gas and time. Very respectfully, I told him thank you, but that I could not buy his house because I did not have any down payment and probably could not afford the mortgage payments. I knew that Menendez and his wife Nereida were trying to help us, but in my mind the idea was not possible.

Menendez, who was a master in finance, had a plan. The value of the home was $25,000. They would sell it to us for the balance of their existing mortgage of $20,000 which we would assume. The mortgage was held by Atlantic Federal Savings and Loan. All we needed was $1,000 to cover closing costs. He had it all arranged with the folks at Atlantic Federal. I was floored by the proposition. I thanked him and told him I was going to talk it over with Yolanda and try to come up with the $1,000. The house had 3 bedrooms and 2 baths, plus a lot of backyard, and it was located across an elementary school. We were at the time paying $145 per month for our apartment, and the new mortgage payment plus taxes and insurance was going to be around $270 per month. After careful consideration we both agreed that we could not pass up this opportunity even though we did not know how we would be able to pay the mortgage, unless I got another par-time job somewhere. The only obstacle left was the $1,000 for the closing costs.

When we told my parents about the deal, they volunteered to lend us the money for the closing costs. I went back to Menendez and I told him that we would do it. He set up the closing day and I helped him move from the old to the new house and then Rene Smith, Yolanda's cousin Terina's husband, helped us move from our apartment to the new house. It was a day with mixed feelings. First I was exhausted after making two moves, second I was worried about the extra expense, and thirdly I was very happy to be able to give my family, especially the children, a better standard of living and room to play and grow. Yolanda's mother, Tete, gave us the living room and the dining room furniture, and we made do with the bedroom furniture that we had. It was like a dream come true for us that we were now owners of our home. Well, together with the bank.

I could not work part-time at Winn Dixie, because it was too far from home now, so I started to give guitar lessons again. I had students that would come to the house and others that I would go to theirs. That little bit helped us, but not enough. Our budget was very tight, and we started to rely on several credit cards that we had, to make ends meet. Not the best financially sound alternative, but temporarily, it helped us. I knew we needed long-term solutions given that very soon we would be faced with educational expenses. Yolanda is masterful when it comes to saving money and she is the great administrator. I gave her complete control of the money and she had her own system of envelopes that worked perfectly. She would have one envelope for each of the monthly expenses. When I got paid, I would cash the check and she would place the money for each expense in the envelope, and that money was not to be touched for anything else. Yolanda would save a lot of money by managing the food expense masterfully. She was already a great cook, and she would not waste any food and always looking for special, and used discount coupons.

Chapter Thirty Three
Getting a College Degree Became a Necessity

As I progressed in my new career, Menendez was giving me more and more responsibilities and he arranged for me to be trained in all the different jobs in his department, so I would act as the backup for sick days and particularly vacations. This was great because, after all my training, I was the only person in the department, outside of Menendez, that was trained in all the jobs. Menendez informed me one day that I was to enroll in his Financial Accounting class. He was a professor in the program called American Institute of Banking (AIB), which was the educational arm of the American Bankers Association. Menendez explained that to continue to grow, I needed more training in accounting. This command was stressful on two counts. First this was difficult and time-consuming material, and second he was the professor and I needed to get a good grade. The bank would pay for the course and the books, and the class was one night per week for 16 weeks. I went through the class; learned a lot and got an "A" thank goodness.

Because I did so well in the course, Menendez recommended that I enroll in more classes, not only to learn more about banking, but also to work towards my Associate Degree at Broward Community College (BCC), today called Broward College. AIB and BCC had a joint program where the students would get both AIB credit towards the four certificates, and also and AA in banking. I told Menendez that I would think about it. I was worried that being busy with school would not allow me to find another part-time job to supplement my salary at the bank. Also, my dislike for school in general was not totally gone from my mind, and I was concerned that I would have too much difficulty studying.

At the time the bank was hiring staff for the management-training program. They would hire college graduates with no banking experience and then put them through an in-house training, and later assign them to branches and departments as officers. Part of their training was to spend several weeks in our department and Menendez gave me the job of conducting the training. After a few of these individuals came through our portion of the training, I had an epiphany. Here I am training these individuals with zero banking experience to later make twice what I was making in salary just because they had a college degree. What was wrong with this picture? I said.

Because I was a service veteran the government through the GI Bill would pay a certain amount for us to go to college. The amount depended on how many credits we took. This payment would come directly to us. I had used about 10 months of the 36 months that I was entitled to, when I went to Florida Computer College, so I had 26 months available. The bank would pay for the courses as long as they were part of the banking or business degree. Given all of these reasons, I decided to enroll in BCC. I love it when you can make one decision and fix several things at the same time. I would get my college education, making myself more "promotable" at the bank, I would learn more about banking and enhance my new career, and last but not least, the additional monies received would act as the part-time job that I needed to make ends meet on our budget.

I started with two classes to test the waters and when I got two A's in them, I then went to three, and later to the maximum of four that I could because they only offered classes at night from Monday to Thursday. This load also qualified me for the maximum payment from the GI Bill. I completed all the requirements for both an Associate in Arts (Banking) with high honors (Above 3.75 GPA) and an Associate in Science (Business) with honors (Above 3.50 GPA). I did the two two-year degrees in three years graduating in August 1974. The situation at the bank was very steady, and I continued to learn more and more from Menendez.

One of the other advantages of taking these banking classes was that I got to know a lot of my fellow bankers. This expanded my limited network of professionals, both with students as well as professors. Among those who I met was Darrell Merkel, who was like me taking banking courses, and we took several courses together. His wife was working at my bank, and he was working at a newly created bank called Bank of Tamarac as a lending officer. One night after class he talked to me about an opportunity at his bank. The new Executive Vice President (EVP) there was looking for someone to run the operations of the bank. This was the same job Menendez had at First National, but on a much smaller scale. I told him that I had never done that job, but that I have had training in most of the components of it. Darrell told me that he knew, from my performance in the classes, that I could do the job and that he was willing to recommend me.

Chapter Thirty Four
Bank of Tamarac the Position Peak of my Banking Career

I saw this as a very good opportunity. I was almost finished with school, and I felt ready and able to take on this challenge. Of course I knew I was not 100% prepared for it, but if one waits to be 100% prepared for anything you want to do, you will never do it. I went to the job interview and found that the EVP was a real nice man with a lot of experience in lending, but very little in operations. He had recently been hired as EVP and Chief Executive Officer (CEO) of the bank and the former CEO and President was going to remain only as an inactive President and board member. This was a fairly new bank with less than one year in existence. The principal owner was Ken Behring who had been the developer of the City of Tamarac and was a very rich man. Regulators grant bank charters based upon, among other things, on the banking experience of its officer and especially the CEO. The original CEO was very old and had many decades of experience, but the board and Mr. Behring now needed a more dynamic leadership and that is why they hired the new EVP and CEO.

The interview went well and I was very honest with him about my experience. He told me that he liked what I told him and that he was ready to offer me the job making $5,000 more per year, a company car, the officer title of Assistant Vice

President (AVP) and Cashier, and free rein in the bank operations. I could not believe this was happening. I had been in banking just over 4 years, I was just a clerk, and I was going to jump to AVP and Cashier of a bank. Of course when I spoke to Yolanda about it we both agreed that I could not pass up this opportunity, but there was still one obstacle. I needed to have Menendez's support for this move because first, I owed him loyalty and respect and would not do anything to hurt him and second, if I was to succeed in this new job, I would need Menendez's support and guidance to get me out of unknown situations and new challenges. I spoke to Menendez and he was very happy for me and told me that I could call him at anytime and that he would help me succeed. Once again this kind and good man was in my corner and ready to continue being my mentor.

The City of Tamarac was largely composed of retirees from the Northeast, mainly from New York. The area was booming with new construction and the bank was poised as a local bank catering to retirees. Many of the new homeowners were directed to the bank by the developer after the closing of their home. The staff was small and the bank was self-contained with the exception of the computer operations, which were handled by First National Bank of Fort Lauderdale, my former bank. This fact gave me an advantage because I was very well trained in all the computer applications and how they impacted the rest of the areas of the bank. I started to get to know all the staff as well as the customers and especially the members of the Board of Directors headed by Mr. Behring, its Chairman.

As time passed, I made some changes, gave some promotions, and hired new staff members. I had several people reporting to me, and we started to have regular weekly meetings to open the lines of communications and work as a team. I loved my job and the challenges of running a very dynamic bank during a very dynamic economic time. The staff, that at first showed some signs of mistrust and lack of confidence in my skills, little by little, as I made the right decisions and provided the right support, began to accept my leadership. I was working very long hours in order to set up all the different procedures and controls that were necessary for a smooth operation. It was at this time that I enrolled in the University of Florida program called Florida School of Banking. This was a non-college credit program of three years where students, all bankers, would go for one week in the summer and then remotely (via regular mail) presented different homework projects every month. This program was co-sponsored by the University and the Florida Bankers Association. It was hard work, but I needed to "beef-up" my resume with additional training. I met a lot of nice people there and I learned a lot.

I started to look for capable and willing staff members so I could delegate some of the tasks as I set them up. I found several who were eager to learn and progress in the bank. I promoted the head teller to Assistant Cashier (Operations Officer), the Assistant Head Teller to Head Teller, a Senior Teller to Assistant Head Teller, the Head Bookkeeper to Assistant Cashier, and hired someone to be the Head Bookkeeper and a new teller. This practice of promoting from within had some really great results and motivated all the staff to work hard because they saw a future. The loan area was supervised by the EVP and CEO with the help of my friend Darrel Merkel the only lending officer. I did not have any experience in loans, so I stayed out of that area mainly because I did not have time, even though I knew that I needed to learn and get involved with loans at some point in my career in order to continue to climb the corporate ladder.

That summer of 1976 my wife, the children, and I took a month vacation. We drove from Plantation Florida up the east coast, and we made several stops along the way. We stopped in Savannah, Georgia, to visit my cousin, Tavito, and his family, we visited Washington DC and all its historical and patriotic locations, we spent a week in New Jersey's West New York visiting Yolanda's niece, Ondinita and then from there visited New York City and all its tourist attractions. 1976 was the bi-centennial year and there were many places that we visited commemorating 200 years of our independence. While we were in West New York, we also visited my aunt, Paquita, and my cousin, Ernesto, who lived in Queens. Ernesto invited us to a show in Radio City Music Hall. We met him there and parked the car in one of the garages. Ernesto came via subway. The show was fantastic and I really enjoyed the Rockettes. After the show I offered to take Ernesto back to his home, but he told me it would be easier if he would go on the subway.

I left the garage and proceeded to go back to West New York, but the more I drove, the more I got lost. I knew I had to find one of the bridges or tunnels to cross the Hudson River towards New Jersey, but I could not. I did not ask anybody on the street for the fear of getting mugged. As we were driving around the area we came into a street were a lot of ladies were standing on the sidewalks. My children started to ask me why these ladies were on the sidewalk and not wanting to explain the real reason these members of the world's oldest profession were out there, I told them that they were cooling off because it was too hot inside their apartments, which was not a total lie after all. The children accepted the explanation and Yolanda and I were relieved. Finally I found a tunnel and crossed the Hudson, then taking Burgerline Avenue I found Ondinita's apartment.

After a few days, we proceeded north toward Canada. We wanted to go to Montreal and Toronto. On the way we stopped at Bear Mountain, which is a beautiful state park situated on the way to Montreal. We got to Montreal around lunchtime, and we had lunch at an authentic French restaurant. There I found out that the Cubans did not invent "flan" as I thought, but that it was actually a French dessert. We visited Mary, Queen of the World Cathedral and a few other places, and we spent the night at a really good hotel. The next morning we headed to Toronto using highway 401, which borders Lake Ontario. This was a really pleasant trip and we stopped several times to admire the views and noticed how clean everything was. It was getting late and I wanted to get to Niagara Falls and sleep there, so we could see the falls at night. I had been there before in 1953 when my parents took my sister and me and I remembered how beautiful it was.

My wife asked me to stop and call a hotel in Niagara Falls and make a reservation because by the time we would get there, according to her, all the rooms would be taken. I did not listen because I thought we could get there in time, but I was wrong. As we approached we could see all the hotels and motels had the signs; "No-Vacancies." We men have a tendency of not listening to our wives and then getting into trouble, and I was no exception. We got to Niagara Falls without a room. We stopped at the shore, so we could see this marvelous spectacle and the children could see how the water would change colors. I told them to wait there by the falls while I would try, on foot, to get us a room. All the nearby hotels were full. Then I went into this hotel, that would have probably been the last chance to get a room, and the clerk gave me the same answer: "No-Vacancies." As I was leaving the desk dejected and sad, the clerk seeing my face told me to wait. "It was close to 10:00 PM" she said: "and we might have something for you." She then proceeded to offer me the "Honeymoon Suite" on the top floor. She told me that she would give me a special price because they were not going to rent it this late, and they would rather have something than nothing for it. I told her that I was not prepared to pay a lot of money, but she gave me a price that even though was double what a regular room would have cost, was almost half their regular charge. I took it and walked back to get my family.

My wife and I were always very conscious of spending too much money, and this trip was going to cost a bundle. Throughout the trip we tried to control expenses, so I decided to play a trick on Yolanda. When I got there I said to her: "I have good news and bad news for you. Which one do you want to hear first?" She told me: "good news." I then said that I have found us a room, but that it was the "Honeymoon Suite" on the top floor. The "bad news" was that it would cost $300 for the night. She was upset and started to give me a lot of "I told you so" sentences. After a few minutes of repri- mands, I said that I was just kidding that it would only cost $100. She smiled and we all went to our room, which had a balcony facing the falls, two bedrooms, and a lot of living space. We had a wonderful time and left the hotel one minute before the checkout time, so we could enjoy every minute of this experience.

Our trip back to Florida took us through the center of the U.S. where we went to a baseball game in Cincinnati and we saw the Big Red Machine team play and beat the Giants. This was a trip none of us have ever forgotten. I felt so happy to be able to provide this experience to my wife and children and was very thankful to God for providing me with a good paying job and a flourishing banking career at the Bank of Tamarac.

One day the EVP and CEO told us that he was leaving the bank and he told me in private that he had recommended me for his job. Now that was a big surprise! That meant that if I was given that job, I would be running the entire bank as EVP and CEO. He told me that in his opinion, I had shown the ability to organize things, implement changes and improvement, and motivate the staff by training them, giving them support, and opportunities for advancement. I was not too sure that I could do this job. A young banker with only a few months of actual operations experience, no lending or investment experience would not be the ideal candidate. Mr. Behring called me to his office and offered me the EVP and CEO job. I accepted it of course and I was given another $5,000 more per year and the reins of the bank. This was 1975, a short 5 years after I started my banking career. This was hard to believe.

One of my first moves was to recommend the promotion of my good friend Darrell Merkel to VP in charge of all the loan functions and made him #2 in the bank. Darrel and I then hired another lending officer who was going to assist Darrel and also take charge of the marketing and business development functions. I then promoted the former Head Teller, now assistant Cashier to AVP and Cashier to run the operations, promoted the former Head Bookkeeper, now assistant Cashier to AVP and Auditor, and promoted others to fill in the positions of those promoted. I had a great team composed of motivated staff members who had advanced through the ranks. The bank continued to grow and passed the regulators examinations with flying colors. We were making money, keeping costs under control, making sound loans, participating and helping the community, and keeping the bank in a very strong liquidity position. Mr. Behring and I played tennis at his house twice per week. He was a great tennis player and fortunately he would win most of the time, and not because I let him. He was actually much better than me.

I became a community leader participating in several community groups, such as the Chamber of Commerce, the Broward County Bankers' Executive Committee, and the Tamarac Symphonic Orchestra, where I was a board member and also preformed as a singer, The Muscular Dystrophy Association as Broward County President, the B'nae B'rith Jewish group, and many others. The intensity of those few months was so great and rewarding that I looked upon those days as the pinnacle of my banking career. You might conclude that I peaked after only five years as a banker. This is sort of déjà vu for me. As a young actor, I had my peak at age 10, now as a young banker I was having my peak at age 32.

Chapter Thirty Five
From Bad to Worse

My career peak was short-lived. Mr. Behring sold his stake in the bank to a former New York City banker, who had retired after making a lot of money and wanted to live in Florida. This man was very different from Mr. Behring. He was not as friendly, and I found him a bit snobbish and pretentious. Mr. Behring was a hands-off owner while the new owner was hands-on. He was not a very good tennis player, so when I played with him, I would sometimes win. Looking back, I should have let him win. One day he asked me to his office and told me that even though I had done a superb job, he was bringing in a President and CEO to run the bank and that I was to remain as EVP and COO (Chief Operating Officer). The new chairman also told me that the new President had a lot of banking experience and above all the needed lending experience that I lacked. He asked me not to go, but to stay because he knew what I had done and how the staff was following me.

At first I was disappointed, to say the least, but I decided to stay and see what this new President was all about. If he was so experienced, maybe I could learn from him, if he was the teaching kind. I spoke to my staff and told them that this decision was for the good of the bank and that for them most things "would remain the same." I needed to say that even if I was not totally convinced it was the truth. When you hear that phrase, you should know that things never remain the same. The new president arrived and we had several meetings with him. He was what most New York bankers would consider to be the "right" type for the job. He was not Cuban, he had a Masters Degree, he had been a banker for over 15 years and he was an experienced lending officer. This new president was a pleasant kind of a fellow. We had several one-on-one and he told me that he could not run the bank without someone like me because he had no prior experience in bank operations or controls.

In the meantime my parents met this banker from Miami at a dinner party. When this banker, who was Cuban, learned that I was a banker also, told my parents to ask me to call him, because as he said it: "Rolandito Ochoa, the banker, should be working for the bank I worked for in Miami and not in Broward." The bank that he worked for, which I will call "Cuban Bank" not to disclose the real name, was also a fairly new bank, less than a year old, and they were looking for someone, who was preferably Cuban, but with U.S. banking operational experience to take over the job of VP and Cashier. When my parents told me, I called this banker for an interview, just in case things did not work out for me at Bank of Tamarac. When I told my wife Yolanda, she did not like it. I had worked in Broward as a banker and never in Miami Dade and she was afraid that I might not like it, plus I would have to commute again. I told her I was going to see what they had to say.

I had also started to talk to my good friend Ricardo (Ricky) Sanchez about the possibility of working with him at Southeast Bank. Southeast Bank was at the time the largest bank in Florida, and Ricky told me that he would help me. Again I was trying to cover different bases in case I needed to make a change. The bigger the bank, the longer it takes to make a hiring decision. Southeast had many banks in Broward as well and maybe after a while I could be transferred and eliminate the long commute. The year was 1976 and we were expecting our number 5 child in early 1977. The other 4 were in Catholic School (Saint Anthony in Fort Lauderdale) and I could not afford to be out of a job for any length of time.

The Cuban Bank made me a job offer basically for the same salary I had at Bank of Tamarac, with a company car and as VP and Cashier. Hindsight is always 20/20. I made the decision to accept the offer mainly driven by my disappointment at Bank of Tamarac, and my fear of having a gap in my cash flow. I gave my resignation at Bank of Tamarac and the president was not happy to see me go and tried to keep me, but I told him that I needed to move on. A member of the staff later told me that he had a heart attack and became disabled. I was sorry to hear that because he was a good man, but not too sorry for the owner of the bank.

Things would have it that going to the "Cuban Bank" was the wrong decision. The bank was in worse conditions than what I was told. There was complete disorganization. There were, I later found out, a lot of politics in the bank and there were basically different groups that "reported" to different "bosses." The person who hired me, who was a director, did it so I could replace the current head of operations who was not in his group. The current head of operations was in the group of the president of the bank, but was never told that I was replacing him. A real soap opera. I started to implement some changes to improve things as I was hired to do. Some of my changes stepped on the toes of, not only the current head of operations, but of others and they complaint to the Chairman of the Board who, was also the CEO.

The chairman came to me one day and, with very nasty and unprofessional vocabulary, asked me why I was making all these changes. I told him that they were needed because the bank was in violation of the law if we continued as before. I told him that it was my impression that I was hired to correct all the violations of the law and regulations as required by the results of the latest examination by the regulators. He was taken aback for an instant by my answer and did not know what to say. He then told me that I was not to make any further changes unless he personally approved them. I was to call him at his business (He was seldom at the bank) and talk to him and that if he was not there, because he was traveling outside the country, I was to leave a message and he would call me back. Needless to say, I was taken aback, but did as I was told. I called the Chairman more than 30 times with items that needed attention, and he never answered back. I called my friend Ricky at Southeast Bank and asked him to try to make it happen there, because I could not stay at this "Cuban Bank."

In the meantime there were many instances where customers of the bank would bring large sums of currency in suit cases to be deposited in the bank. Back then the regulations governing currency transactions (Bank Secrecy Act) were not as strict as they are today, but nevertheless these transactions could only lead to further deterioration of the bank's relations with the regulators and other authorities. If I was in charge of operations, these transactions fell under my control, and I did not want to be involved in any scandal in the future. Ricky came through for me and I was offered a position at Southeast Bank of Tamiami as VP and Cashier.

After less than 3 months, I rendered my resignation to the person that had hired me in the first place. He was very upset because my resignation included a list of all the items that needed to be changed, the date that I called the Chairman and the fact that he never called me back in any of them. The Chairman, at the time, was out of the country on business, so the person who hired me and another influential director invited me to dinner at a fancy restaurant on Brickell Avenue to try to persuade me to stay. I accepted the invitation and had a really great dinner. When we were finished and after I told them everything that I was told not to do, and needed to be done, this influential director who was also the bank's attorney, asked me: "How much would it take for you to stay?" I looked at him squarely in the eyes and said: "There is not enough money to keep me here." Then he said: "Then there is nothing else we need to discuss." We said goodbye and I thanked them for their actions.

I had given them 2 weeks to find a replacement, and they accepted that. While I was wrapping this up, I saw a good friend of mine coming in for an interview for my job. After he finished, I called him over and gave him a copy of my resignation letter and told him: "Only take the job if they agree to make all these changes." He was hesitant to use my letter, but I told him that he could use it because it could benefit him and the bank. He accepted the position and was in it for more than 30 years thereafter. As a side note, this bank was in a legal battle and scandal not too long after I left, due to the same items I wanted to change. My friend, who took over my job, had not had the time to make all the changes and he had to battle through those difficult days, but at the end he fixed everything and the bank is now strong and well run.

Chapter Thirty Six
Southeast Bank: A good career move

Southeast Bank was a holding company which owned many different single unit banks in Florida. One of these unit banks was Southeast Bank of Tamiami located on SW 8 Street and 122 Avenue in Miami. The original location is now Wells Fargo Bank. The Florida Legislature passed a law in 1975 (effective January 1, 1977), which allowed branch banking in Florida. When I started in late 1976 each of the unit banks owned by the holding company operated with a separate board of directors and had its president and all the other officers. There were many benefits obtained by the holding company model such as centralization of computer systems, human resources, purchasing, and others. In essence the unit banks operated as if they were branches, but kept the necessary structure to comply with the law.

I was hired as VP and Cashier to replace my friend Ricardo (Ricky) Sanchez who was promoted to VP of Lending. The president was a Canadian by the name of Victor Raymond. The bank was also newly opened and the area was sparsely developed. We had two large customers; Florida International University (FIU) and the Miccosukee Tribe of Indians. The area was growing by leaps and bounds and it was a very busy bank. My friend, Ricky, helped me a lot not only with the details of the job, but also teaching me the corporate culture, and above all, the gift of his friendship that has lasted until today.

Ricky was and still is one the most respected lending officers in the Miami banking circles. He has hundreds of loyal customers that he has cultivated and served with utmost care and professionalism. We had met a few years before at a Catholic Church movement called "Impactos." Ricky was one of the founders of this movement, that is a weekend exercise for couples with small children. Yolanda and I participated with our four children in Impacto #8 and later on the team of several Impactos. Ricky, at the tender age of 17, had participated as a paratrooper in the Bay of Pigs invasion on April 1961. He was captured, sent to jail, and later liberated in the exchange that the U.S. negotiated with Castro where Castro got medicines and the U.S. got the troops that they had abandoned. I was very lucky to be his friend and to have him as my mentor during my first years at Southeast Bank.

Our fifth child Robert Miguel Ochoa was born on January 17, 1977 at Plantation General Hospital. Robert was a beautiful baby, and for the first time I was able to be in the delivery room and experience the miracle of birth first-hand. I also witnessed the difficulty mothers experienced when they have a baby. My mother, who had had kidney stones, always used to say that giving birth was twice as painful as kidney stones. Yolanda and I had gone through the training program for natural birth, and I was ready to be the best coach. The delivery went without any problems, and we were leaving the hospital the next day. When I went to pick them up in the morning we were encountered by a very unusual phenomenon. It was snowing in Plantation. Yes, January 18, 1977 brought us snow flurries. This has not happened since. Robert was baptized at Saint George Catholic Church shortly thereafter.

While I was at Southeast Bank of Tamiami I experienced two extremely unusual and personally traumatic events. The first event took place on a very busy Friday afternoon. Back then before direct deposit of payroll, Fridays were extremely busy because everyone needed to go to the bank and cash their payroll checks for the weekend. The bank was crowded inside and out at the drive-in and the lines were very long. Customers would get upset because they had to wait a few minutes. I was always on the lookout for things I could do to try to expedite the customers' transactions. I learned that from our president, Mr. Raymond, who would go through the customers in line approving transactions so when they got to the teller's window it would go faster. Ricky and I used to do it in the drive-in. We would go out with pens and deposit slips and asked the customers in line to prepare their transaction before they got to the window.

That Friday in question was no exception. We were crazy with customers all over the place. The clerk who handled the safe deposit area came to me with an unusual transaction. The owner of the safe deposit box had died, and her husband presented a court order to get access to it. The clerk did not read the order and just gave it to me for my approval since the husband was not an authorized signer. I hardly read the order, and due to the craziness of the moment, approved it without fully reading it. The husband was given access to the box. We went through the rest of the day and went home for the weekend. First thing Monday morning the son of the deceased and his lawyers were at the bank with a similar court order. The clerk brought it to me for approval. As I was reading it, this time completely, I felt sick, as my blood seemed to leave my body. The order was not to allow access to the box, but ordering an inventory of the contents. I had made a terrible error in allowing the husband, not the father of the son, to have unrestricted access to the box. I accompanied the son and his lawyer to the box to find it empty.

I immediately communicated my error to Mr. Raymond and Ricky. They spoke to the son's lawyer who threatened to sue the bank. Mr. Raymond communicated with the auditing and the security departments and started an investigation. They also notified the bank's attorney. Because the banks do not know what is in the boxes, this suit could allege that large amounts of valuables were in the box, and we had no way to prove otherwise. I was in a real pickle and I had placed the bank in a very vulnerable position with my actions. I thought that the correct thing to do was to resign before I got fired. I prepared a resignation letter and gave it to Mr. Raymond. He read it and told me that I was taking the easy way out, and he was going to give me a chance to solve it and keep my job. If I could do it in three day, I would keep my job. If I did not, he would accept my resignation. I thanked him, but said to him: "How am I going to solve this?" He said in turn: "Get the stuff from the box back from the husband."

I went back to my desk to think and plan what I was going to do. First I found out that the husband was the owner of the general store, that served the Miccosukee tribe, so I rode my car to the store. As I went in the store I confronted the owner (husband) with a strong approach. I told him that what he had done was against the law and that unless he returned all the contents of safety deposit box immediately, the bank would press charges. He looked at me and said: "I have nothing to return so you, damm Cuban, get out of my store." I got out and drove back to the bank and informed Mr. Raymond the results of my visit. Mr. Raymond said: "You still have 2 more days."

Of course that night I could not sleep thinking about it. How could I have been so careless? How could I have not read that order completely? How could I have allowed this error to ruin my career in banking? The next morning I was at the general store very early. As I entered the owner told me to get out. I asked him to listen to me for a moment. Now I used the soft approach. I explained to him how hard I had worked for many years to build up my career and this event was going to ruin it. I also explained to him that I had 5 children to feed and that if I lose my job they will go hungry. As I said that, I started to cry. This was not an act. The fact that I was a nervous wreck and with almost no sleep the night before, made it easy to get emotional. The owner looked at me with a blank stare and said: "I have nothing to return so you, damm Cuban, get out of my store." I got out and drove back to the bank and informed Mr. Raymond the results of my visit. Mr. Raymond said: "You still have 1 more day."

The next morning after again no sleep the night before, I got to my desk in the morning with nothing left to do than start packing my belongings and leave. As the bank opened at 9:00 AM, who came through the doors if not the husband with a paper bag in his hand. He came to my desk and told me he was returning the contents of his deceased wife's deposit box. I sat there motionless for a few seconds. Was it the soft approach that worked or maybe the strong approach needed to sink in? I would never know the answer, but at that point it did not matter. I called Mr. Raymond over and the three of us did an inventory of the contents. We contacted our attorneys who told us to prepare a release/affidavit for the husband to sign. I was surprised to see that nothing of value was in the contents. The deceased lady only had papers, photos, and the title to her car, but no tangible valuables. We proceeded to call the son who arrived there shortly. We also prepared a release/affidavit for him to sign and we put all the contents in our vault under dual control to await the court's decision. Thanks to Mr. Raymond I had saved my job, but more importantly the lesson served me for the rest of my career. I never sign or approve any paper especially a court order, without first fully reading it and understanding it.

The other event that took place during my years at Southeast Bank of Tamiami was a lot different, but as personally traumatic as the first one. During those days (late 70s) bank regulations were not as they are today as far as money laundering is concerned. Today it is virtually impossible for a bank employee or officer to fudge the records and look the "other way" while a customer makes a large currency transaction (More than $10,000). The computer systems today have strict control. If a large currency transaction is made, an automatic report is generated to the Internal Revenue Service. During the late 70s and early 80s, it was fairly easy to look "the other way." One afternoon a very clean-cut and Hispanic-looking man approached my desk and sat down. He proceeded to offer me a deal. He would pay me 2% commission under the table for every large currency transaction that I did not report and look "the other way." He knew the system and knew that as the person in charge of operations, I had to manually sign every IRS-4789 form that the tellers would generate after these transactions happened. It would have been very easy for me to just destroy the form given that there was no automatic tracking done.

At the time I was financially stripped given the five children, four of them in parochial school, and one more on the way. I was teaching in the banking program, giving guitar lessons, and doing anything to make ends meet for us. The offer was very tempting for a few seconds. My ethical, religious, and moral standards would not let me do it. As a professional banker with my eyes on a future more successful career, that could also be ruined by this act, I had to think fast as to what I was going to say, because you do not want to upset these people because they have the tendency to be violent and unforgiving. I explained to the man that he had chosen the wrong individual because I was basically a coward and if I did it, everyone would know because I would be so nervous that I would ruin the entire operation. I thanked him for the offer and he got up and walked towards the front door.

Back in those days we did not have the video equipment that we have today. We relied on photo cameras that needed to be activated either by an alarm or manually from a button on each of the desks and teller stations. As the man was walking toward the front door, I took several pictures of him with the camera mounted on top of the door. The training that I had received in security took over my instincts at that moment and gave me the presence of mind to take those pictures. Then I sat at my desk for a few minutes pondering what to do next. I had two alternatives: report the incident to my superiors and the security department or say nothing and go about my job as if nothing had happened. The first would be what is expected of me as an officer of the bank, but could have negative repercussions on my safety and that of my family. The second could be disastrous if this person was a "plant" from the government or from the bank and I did not properly report it. This is what is called an ethical dilemma when all the alternatives have some negative consequences. My parents always insisted that I tell the truth and that the truth would always liberate you. So I went to Mr. Raymond's office and made the report.

In a matter of minutes the bank was full of FBI agents, internal security people, and auditors. I was interviewed by two or three different people and one of them asked if I had taken pictures. I told him yes, and then they proceeded to take the film out of the camera, had it developed, and showed it to me for proper identification. I was so scared! I did identify the man and after that my life was miserable for many months to come. I told my wife and she was understandably hysterical and very concerned for the safety of the children. I asked her to be alert and to take different routes when she took the children to school. I took different routes too and I looked under my car every time I was going to insert the key in the door. This lasted for a few months and fortunately nothing happened and I never knew the outcome of the investigation. That was a good thing! This event confirmed my belief that no matter how difficult things are, you have no excuse to act unethically or illegally.

Southeast Bank was the largest Holding Company in Florida at the time and had the latest computer systems as well as great training programs. After I was there a while, I asked to participate in the credit-training program. I knew I needed to obtain more training in lending and going through this highly prestigious training, would be the first step. I was granted permission to participate and successfully completed the program. After that, Ricky started to train me in actual lending and this was the beginning of my lending career.

Southeast Banks was "big" on training. They continued to support my attendance to the Florida School of Banking. I learned a lot from it, and I was able to apply that knowledge at my job after my graduation in August 1977. I also asked to be sent to the Commercial Lending School at the University of Oklahoma located in Norman. This program sponsored by the American Banking Association, was for two-weeks straight and was directly focused on commercial or business loans.

This knowledge was immediately applied in my job after my graduation in May 1977, and was extremely useful during the rest of my banking career. This move was also done to try to compensate for my lack of a bachelors degree.

During that time I also started my teaching career. I started teaching in the Dade County Adult Education Program, which was a combined effort with the Miami Chapter of the American Institute of Banking (AIB). Ricky was also asked to teach and we did it for a few years. I later started teaching through AIB directly several different banking courses. These courses were taught at different bank locations. The extra income helped me obtain added cash flow for our home expenses, which included tuition at Saint Anthony School, where our children attended from first to eight grade. Around that time I started to teach guitar lessons again. I had several students, and for the most part, I would go to their homes after work on the nights when I did not teach classes.

As mentioned before, I love the game of baseball, but I knew that I could not play it anymore so I turned to the game of softball. I started playing while I was still living in Miami at a pick-up game we had Saturdays at Saint Michael's Church. Then I played on a team we formed for the catholic league called: Damascos. While I was working at First National Bank of Fort Lauderdale, I played on their team in a local league. Because this pick-up game was getting really good as far as the quality of the players who were starting to come, one of the players who was the owner of a business in Coconut Grove, came up with the idea to select the best players and form a team to play in the already formed "Liga Cubana." This league was the strongest in Miami and played on Sundays at Curtis Park located in NW 20th Street. The name of the team was Grove Furriers, which was the name of the business that was sponsoring it. The owner the company and coach was Alfonso Zequeira who was a great enthusiast of the game.

I played shortstop and was hitting at the top of the order. We did pretty well and one year we were in the playoffs. We went to the finals against the team from Navarro's Pharmacies. In that decisive game we were losing 4 to 3 in the bottom of the 7th and last inning. The top of the order was due and our first hitter hit a two-base hit. The next hitter was out on a fly and then it was my turn to hit. I hit a very high fly to left field and the left fielder known by the nickname "Bandido" was waiting for the ball with his back to the fence. Bandido jumped to try to catch the ball that was going out for a home run, the ball hit the tip of his glove, but he could not retain it and I had a home run, and we won the game and the championship. This was a very exciting moment and I was filled with pride and happy to be successful in a sport I really liked.

We continued to play in the Liga Cubana (Cuban League), but never won the championship again. I changed from shortstop to pitcher and was doing quite well until a game in the playoff against a very good team. We were winning by one run in the last at bat of the opposing team and I then decided, in my head, that I could not throw a strike. I walked the bases loaded and then walked the tying run in. The more I tried to throw strikes the more balls I threw. My mental block was getting the best of me. Alfonso came to talk to me and I asked to be replaced, but he told me that he was sure I could do it because the next hitter was their pitcher who was a very poor hitter. Alfonso said that if I pitched to him just a soft pitch as a strike, he could only hit a fly or a grounder in the infield and that he would never hit for a run batted in. I agreed with him and started to pitch to this weak hitter who was not swinging at anything. I took him to a full count of three balls and two strikes and then I threw another ball walking him and losing the championship. That was one of the worst moments in my sports career, and I felt bad that I had let my teammates down; which goes to show that in sports, especially softball, anything can happen and one day you are a hero and the next a bum.

Some years went by and then I started to play on a different league called: "Liga de La Libertad." (Liberty League) This league played at Tamiami Park and had very strong teams. My wife and children accompanied me to the games and we tried to make this a family outing, which was not too expensive. On this team I was the pitcher and one year we went to the playoffs. The night before, it had been raining and the field was very slippery. As I was pitching my left foot slipped in the mud and I felt a real strong pain in my lower back. It was obvious that I was hurt, but very stupidly I continued to pitch a few more innings and we won the game. The following Saturday was the final and we were in it. I went home and was in real pain. My wife insisted that I go to the hospital or the doctor to have this injury looked at, but I did not listen to her.

The desire to pitch the final game got the best of me and I spent the entire week putting ice and heat on my lower back and taking aspirin. Nothing worked and the pain was still there Friday night. My wife said to me: "You are not thinking of pitching tomorrow?" Again I did not listen. I got up very early on Saturday and took white tape and made like a corset for my entire lower back. That made me feel a little better because of its support. I went to the game, pitched, and we won the game and the championship, but on Monday I could not walk and was taken to the hospital where they have to put me in traction. The doctor said that I had a split disk in the lumbar area and also second-degree burns on my skin due to the white tape that I put against the skin with no gauze in between. I learned several lessons here. First, listen to my wife, second, my health is more important than winning the game, third, do not put white tape against the skin, and finally that I would have to live with back pain the rest of my life.

Also in 1978 I was fortunate to be asked to participate as a member of the Federal Reserve Bank of Miami Electronic Funds Transfer System (EFTS) Steering Committee. The group was composed of mainly computer operations experts, a few line bankers, such as myself, with some former computer experience, and Federal Reserve Bank senior operational individuals. This group was charged with exploring the alternatives for the future of electronic banking. All the electronic services that we enjoy today, were back them just a "dream" on the minds of the committee members. I was one of only two Cubans on the committee and for that I was proud.

After a few meetings, and when I started to understand more about the future, I asked the chair of the committee and the other members if they had studied what effect the elimination of float would have in the economy and in the ability for banks to lend money. When I asked that question, all the members looked at each other and then looked at me as if I were from another planet. Not a single member on the committee had an economics background or monetary policy experience. I had had some courses in Economics and I understood well how banks make money by lending. I also knew that the float (funds in transit from one bank to the other and not yet available to the customer) was a large part of the pool of funds that banks use for lending. Think of it as the banks were lending funds that were not there. The amount of the U.S. economy Money Supply is composed of currency in circulation and checking account deposits in commercial banks.

In 1979 the mix of the two components was 27.7% for currency and 72.3% for checking account deposits. By June 2005, after the full implementation of electronic clearing of checks, the mix of the two components was 51.6% currency and 48.4% checking account deposits. There were many reasons for the economic meltdown of 2007, but I think that the full implementation of electronic clearing of checks contributed to the crisis in a significant way. First, the value of the dollar was reduced by the increment of its supply. In addition, banks lacked liquidity to make commercial loans and turned to mortgage loans, which they could sell in the secondary market and then re-invest in new mortgage loans. Most of you know the "rest of the story." In my humble opinion this was the beginning of the domination of the businesses in the U.S. and most of the world by the technical staff (Techies) and away from the business people. There is no stopping this "progress" now.

Chapter Thirty Seven
Southeast Bank: The beginning of the metamorphosis in banking

Most of the large bank holding companies in Florida have started to change their organizational structure from a "unit bank" model to a "branch banking" model. This new model allowed bank holding companies in Florida to gradually convert unit banks to branches. The new laws started by allowing bank holding companies to only have branches in counties were they had the unit bank. Later that was expanded to adjacent counties, and finally to the entire state. These changes eliminated a lot of the middle management jobs, a lot of the top management jobs, as well as many support positions. A unit bank needed to have all the components of a bank while a branch only needed the customer contact positions, because all the branches could be supported and managed in a centralized mode.

In mid 1978 Southeast Banks started to make this conversion. My job as VP and Cashier would eventually disappear. The new business model only needed one VP and Cashiers for each county and eventually for the entire state. Dade County was the largest for Southeast, so they did it last. I started to get a little concerned about my future so I asked for an appointment with Anthony Infante who was now our president. Mr. Infante was for many years the largest producer and money-maker for the entire holding company when he was the president of the unit called: Southeast Bank of Coral Gables. As Southeast was getting ready to implement the structural changes, they made him the president of several units and relocated the displaced presidents into other positions. Mr. Infante was rumored to be the selection for the position of president for the entire bank once it was totally converted. He was an outstanding banker with a tremendous knowledge of the Dade County market where most of the deposits and loans were housed. He knew how to run a bank profitably and efficiently.

I went to the appointment with Mr. Infante to ask him if he knew what my future would be with the bank. I wanted to hear it from him before I started to look for alternatives. To my surprise, Mr. Infante, who was an extremely friendly and positive individual, told me the following: "If I do not know what the #### is going to happen to me, how would I know what is going to happen to you?" I was surprised and taken aback. When I told Ricky, who knew Infante better than me, he told me that it sounded like Infante was not getting the top job. I was quite disappointed and worried about my future. I loved working for Southeast and I loved my unit, my staff, and my customers. Southeast, the great bank that it was had many open positions posted at the time and I applied for an Assistant Manager position at Broward County Deerfield Beach Branch. I went to the interview and I got the position so I was transferred in the middle of 1979.

As a side note, Mr. Infante was not made the bank's president and he left Southeast and opened his own bank. He took with him a lot of his customers as well as his staff. The individual who was named president of the bank was an Anglo from the Orlando area who had little knowledge of the South Florida market. Some, including me, thought that the main reason Mr. Infante was not selected had to do with prejudice. The board of directors and the larger stockholders of the bank were all Anglo and they saw Southeast Bank as an Anglo bank. Naming a Cuban as the top officer would have been very difficult at the time. Cubans were making big strides during those years, but there were still a lot of mistrust and prejudices, which as the years have gone by, have diminished. Southeast started to lose market given that other bank holding companies have reacted to the increase of importance of the Cuban market in South Florida and had placed Cubans in top positions. Also many smaller banks were opened with Cuban ownership. Southeast continued its vision that excluded many of the Cuban businesses and emphasized international transactions. When the South Florida local economy dipped the bank failed on September 19, 1991 and was taken over by the FDIC and sold to First Union, now Wells Fargo. What would have happened if Mr. Infante would have been named president? I guess we will never know.

My new position was very similar with the exception of the accounting and investment part of the job. This branch had been a very successful unit and had more than $100 Million in deposits and over 30 staff members. I was in charge of all tellers, new accounts, customer service, safe deposit, and vault operations. It was a very difficult time because the unit banks had been transitioned into branches and many of the staff members were not used to the new model. This was a step back as far as my lending career, because I was not involved with the lending function whatsoever. There were many old-time staff members who had a hard time getting used to a new boss and a new model. Among them was a customer service officer who had been there the longest. Her claim to fame was that she was "friends" with the newly selected bank president.

She would drop his name all the time as if trying to intimidate those around her, including the branch manager and me. She was actually very lazy and did little work. In the old model, she survived, but in the new model, she needed to step-up to the plate and do some work. I had several meetings with her and assigned different tasks, which she did not do. I spoke to the manager in anticipation of her performance review and mentioned that she might not be too happy with it. The manager reviewed it and made some minors changes to soften the blow, but is was still quite negative.

She was really upset with me after her rating went almost to the lowest level. She spoke to the manager, to human resources, and of course to her friend, the new president. She asked to be transferred to the lending area were the supervisor was her long-time friend and I was delighted to replace her and to be able to hire someone who could contribute to the branch in a positive way. Even though this confrontation created some heat for me, the overall results were very positive. All the other staff members reporting to me fell into one of two groups: Those who did not like her and were glad I did it and those who thought that they had better dance to my music if they wanted to stay. The results were positive and I had the support of most of my staff.

While at this branch our sixth child Joseph Richard Ochoa was born on March 19, 1979 at Plantation General Hospital. I also participated as a coach for Yolanda's delivery. This time it was not very easy because Joseph weighted over 9 and one half pounds and also his chord was in the way. After a few tense moments, he was born. He was a beautiful baby. We actually were not in agreement about his name. I wanted to call him Joseph or Jose, but Yolanda did not. My mother was named Josefina in my grandfather on my mother's side was named Jose. Yolanda did not want him to later be called "Pepito." Pepito is a character in many of the Cuban jokes. Sometimes these jokes are a little off-color. So when he was born on March 19, Saint Joseph's Day, the matter was settled. We made a conscious decision to call him Joey to eliminate the possibility of "Pepito." Joey was baptized shortly thereafter at Saint George Catholic Church.

As our family grew, and we were faced with additional expenses, I started to teach at Broward Community College in the American Institute of Banking (AIB) program. This was the same dual-credit program from which I graduated. At the time I could teach with the credentials I had and my years of experience. Most of the classes were given at night and the classrooms were located in different banks in the area. This activity provided more financial support for our family and helped us fulfill our desire that our children attend a Catholic school. My salary from the different banks I had worked in the last five years had remained leveled, so I had to find added support to face the ever-increasing expenses.

In order to further my efforts and increase the family's income, I came up with an idea to help me do so. During those days in Miami bring-your-own-bottle (BYOB) parties were very popular and there was no such activity in Broward County. There were, in my estimation, enough Cubans and other Hispanics in Broward at the time to support such an activity and I decided to test that concept and see what happened. I started searching for a hall or any other building, which would be appropriate for this activity. There were not very many, but I found one that was well located and reasonably priced.

I started this process just after our son Joey was born in March 1979. The overall economy was very weak and we had had many years of inflation and very high interest rates. The price of gasoline was around $0.86 per gallon. The country was engulfed in a fuel crisis due to many factors, which included the situation in Iran where the Shah (Mohammad Reza Pahlavi) had left with his family on January 16, 1979. Would these economic conditions affect the results of my small entrepreneurship adventure? I thought not. I concluded that people needed to have fun and entertained themselves no matter what was happening.

I went ahead and closed the contract with the U.S. Army Reserve Armory hall located on State Road 84 in Fort Lauderdale near I-95 and other important arteries. This location was near Port Everglades and the airport. I set the date for June 30, 1979. I then started looking for the elements needed for a successful BYOB party: Good access and parking, good music, some food items, and an entertaining program of activities during the party. I had good access and parking in the Armory, so that was solved.

Next I needed to find the best possible music so I contacted Carlos Oliva, who at the time not only had his own musical group, Los Sobrinos del Juez, but was also an agent for many other groups. My first choice was a band that at the time was at the top of all dance bands in South Florida namely "Miami Sound Machine." I explained to Carlos the idea and asked him if it would be possible for the band to perform and share 50% of the take after expenses. This was the only way I could bring such a high caliber band and attract the audience at the same time, not put a financial burden on me in case things did not work out well. It is always important to try to cover the downside. Carlos agreed. Then I contracted my good friend Roly Rodriguez, who was at the time one of the premier disc jockeys in the area to provide the music when the band would take breaks. We came to an agreement and Roly also provided the sound system for the band.

The next step was to find a source for finger food and soft drinks and for that I contacted our Cuban butcher, who agreed to bring these items at no cost to me. He would profit all the sales. This also eliminated expenses for me. The next items I needed were to get chairs and tables given that the Armory did not have them. I contacted the pastor of my parish and asked him to rent some of the parish's chairs and tables. I offered him a donation. I did the same for the principal of the kid's school and I now had all that I needed. The day of the event, I would rent a truck, pick the chairs and tables up at the two locations and then with the help of my wife and older children set them up in the Armory.

At this point I had everything lined up so I started the promotional phase. I had printed tickets, posters, and flyers and started to contact several local Cuban businesses and asked them to display the poster and also sell the tickets. For their help, I gave them two free tickets. I was able to get several who were willing to display the poster and three who were willing to sell the tickets. I also mailed a letter to all of my friends and contacts in Broward County and contacted them by phone a few days after. I could have used the Internet, but we did not have that at the time.

The Armory had a capacity of 500 people and my break-even analysis showed that I needed 250 to break even. Slowly I started to sell tickets and as the days passed I started to get nervous. Many people told me that they were worried about the economy and what was happening and they could not go. Many told me that they had not made the decision yet and that they were going to wait. This practice of not making long-term decisions is very common in the Hispanic community.

Then something happened that hurt this effort the most. "An organization called Florida Independent Truckers Rights Association, called a strike which stopped all deliveries of gasoline from Port Everglades. The entire economy of South Florida was about to be brought to its knees as 1,500 service stations were out of gasoline. Governor Bob Graham declared South Florida to be in a disaster emergency. He called in 1,800 National Guardsmen to transport the fuel with Florida Highway Patrol escorts." (http://www.flhsmv.gov/fhp/history/1970s.htm)

The mobilization of the National Guard one week before the party put the availability of the Armory at risk because all the guardsmen were stationed there during this operation. I contacted the person in charge at the Armory and he could not give me any assurances or dates. My party was up-in-the-air and everyone knew it, so the sale of tickets came to a screeching halt. I was ready to cancel it, but waited to see what happened. Two days before the event the guard mobilization was stopped and the Armory was available and I was by contract obligated to pay the rent with or without the party. Given that the largest expense was already committed, I decided to go ahead with it knowing that it would be a financial failure. We tried to make a last ditch effort over the phone to get people to go, but the damage was done.

That day we set up everything and were ready to "party." The attendance was 140, far from the 250 needed to break-even and very far from an attendance that would give Miami Sound Machine the earnings that they commanded at the time. Carlos Oliva was there that day and saw what was happening and as the gentleman that he is, told me not to worry that in business "sometimes you win and sometimes you lose." On the other hand the party was a success. Everyone who showed up had a wonderful time. Why wouldn't they? We had the best band, the best DJ, great location, ample room to dance, adequate food and drinks, and many other amenities such as dance contests, a live show by my father, Rolando Ochoa, who performed several of his famous monologues. At the end everyone who went congratulated me for such a great party and many suggested that I must do it again. I was devastated knowing that after all these efforts, instead of helping to increase my family's income; I had decreased it by over $1,500 dollars.

After the party we picked up all the tables and chairs and the next day delivered them to the church and school. I returned the rental truck and the next day I was in the hospital with one of my many split disc episodes. The heavy lifting and the stress of the experience had provoked the pain. I was there for several days. Once I was out, I did a complete analysis of the financial results and decided to meet with Carlos Oliva and give him a check out of my own money to compensate, in a small way, the efforts and the talent of Miami Sound Machine. Carlos refused the check for $300.00, but accepted it after my strong insistence. Looking back and maybe the only "silver lining" for this experience was the fact that I was able to "hire" one of the most famous bands in the world, with one of the top pop singers of all time, Gloria Estefan, for only $300.00.

While at the Deerfield branch of Southeast Bank I also experienced a very unusual event related to safe deposit boxes. Because this branch had been a very old bank before, we had a very large safe deposit area with many boxes. We were very close to many retirement communities in Deerfield Beach and retirees love their safe deposit boxes. It gives them something to do and a reason to come to the bank and fill part of the day.

We had two clerks who staffed this department and we had more than 50 entries a day and many more Fridays and Mondays. Fridays, the lady customers would come in to take out their favorite jewels for the weekend and on Mondays to put them back. One of these busy days we had the visit of the husband of one of our customers who was accompanied by a lady who pretended to be his wife. This couple had separate boxes and neither one was authorized to enter the other's box. Both attendants knew the husband well because he used to come often. The real wife did not visit her box regularly. The fake wife had the key to the box and she was introduced by the husband as his wife.

In this branch we had an unusual system. The owner of the box must sign the entry card as it is in most safe deposit departments, but in addition we would take a picture of the person visiting with a camera that had two lenses. One that took the face and the other looking down, took the signed entry card. The fake wife signed the card, but the attendant did not check the files to make sure it was the same and then took the fake wife's picture. They went in together and after a few minutes came out with a bag full of contents. A few hours later, the real wife came in and went in her box coming out quickly saying: "As I expected, my box is empty. Someone has been there without my permission and took everything." Of course the attendant brought the real wife to me and she was really upset. She explained that her husband and her were getting divorced and that he did this to steal her valuables. I called our attorneys and let them know what was going on.

In the meantime I remembered that we had taken a picture of perpetrator and the husband and I told the wife. She then asked me if she could get a copy of the picture and if she did she would not press charges against the bank. After consulting with our attorneys, I had the picture developed and the wife came back for her copy. I had prepared a release/affidavit for her to sign. When she saw the picture her eyes light up and thanked me, signed the document and went on her way. We later found out that she had shown the picture to the husband and used it to have him return everything to her and also to forgo any other assets that they had. If he would have refused, she would press criminal charges against him and his girl-friend. Of course he accepted the deal and came out with nothing from the divorce because she was the one with the money. We had to let go the attendant and I escaped one more time the danger of safe deposit boxes. After that I stayed away from them as much as I could.

My first supervisor in banking, Manuel Fernandez Grande, was also working for Southeast Bank. He had been in charge of the computer operations at First National Bank in Fort Lauderdale and was now in charge of the operations for a region that included Broward, Palm Beach and Martin Counties. Manuel was an experienced banker from Cuba who also had a long history of service to Cuba. During the Batista dictator-ship, he conspired against it and was part of an underground group in Havana. After a couple of years after the rise of Cas-tro, Manuel realized that Castro was worse and started to con-spire against the revolution. He held positions of leadership with the group called "30 de Noviembre" (30th of November). He is a great leader and his style of supervision inspired some of the tactics I used in my banking career.

One of Manuel's main duties at Southeast was to coordi-nate the training, conversion, and support for all the bank's acquisitions that Southeast bank was doing at the time. South-east was purchasing smaller banks throughout the state and converting them into branches in the system. We saw each other at a bank meeting and he asked me to be part of his team. He needed someone with knowledge of computers, training, and bank operations to coordinate the absorption of these banks into Southeast. I accepted the position of Manager of Conversions and New Projects for the region. My duties included forming a training team, coordinating the conversion into our computer system, and providing support to the new staff after the conversion.

This was an exciting position where I interacted with not only the members of the team, but also with Southeast Bank's new employees. I was given a large blue van to be able to transport the team to the different locations. Once there, we would train the new employees on the new system that they would be using after conversion. We then set up the date for the conversion which was normally on Friday night so we would have time to make any corrections over the weekend. On Monday morning we would be at each location to provide guidance and support and remain there for about a week. I was involved with this position until the first part of 1981. I really enjoyed working with Manuel and his team and we started a friendship that lasts until today.

In 1980 I ran for the office of Chapter Treasurer for the American Institute of Banking (AIB) for Broward County. I won the election and began a 5-year commitment guiding the operations of this educational institution. Every year a new treasurer would be elected and each of the officers would move up the ranks: First to VP of Education, then to President elect, then to President, and finally to Past President. The board would direct the operations of the chapter and the fund raising and community events. During those years I felt I was giving back some of the good things that I had received from AIB.

Chapter Thirty Eight
Sun Bank of Broward:
Back to the customers

Due to my involvement with AIB, I attended many of their functions and events. It was a great way to maintain business contacts and it afforded me opportunities for networking. A countywide tennis tournament was one of those occasions. I was playing for the Southeast Team and saw many of my friends and former colleagues from previous banks and previous AIB classes. Among them was John Morris. John Morris had worked with me at First National Bank of Fort Lauderdale where he was a senior lending officer, but more importantly he was my AIB professor for a very difficult class called Analyzing Financial Statements. He had been a very demanding professor, but at the same time he was a great individual with ample knowledge and an acute sense of humor. Many admired John Morris and he was also an accomplished musician playing the French Horn.

John and I started to talk and he asked me what I was doing and I told him. He asked me if I was happy and I answered yes and no. Yes, because I liked what I was doing and I enjoyed working for Manuel, but no, because my salary at Southeast had hardly increased during the almost five years of my career there. Some of the events that took place during this time were to be blamed for this lack of financial progress, but some had to do with a deteriorating trend at Southeast. Southeast used to be where everyone wanted to work because they took care of their employees and they had very good benefits. The changes in the structure, plus the inflation experienced in the late 70s had made getting a raise almost impossible.

John was working for Sun Bank of Broward as its Executive VP in charge of Branch Administration. He told me that he had an opening for a Branch Manager at their Tamarac East Branch and wanted to know if I would be interested in applying for it. I always explored the possibilities that come my way and I sent him my resume as soon as possible. He called me back for an interview with the president of the bank. I went to the interview with the president whose first name was Charlie. He was what we call a "good old boy" who spoke with frankness and with a very heavy southern accent. He went through my resume and asked me several questions. I sensed that he was satisfied with my answers and I felt good about how the interview was going. Charlie then sat back in his chair and told me: "I am going to ask you a question and I want you to answer it sincerely. Do you think a Cuban will be able to work with all the Jews in Tamarac? At first I was taken aback at this very illegal question, but instead of taking offense to it, I tried to answer it as he had asked me to do, sincerely.

First I reminded him that I had worked in Tamarac before and that I was very much accepted by the Jewish community and secondly I told him that a person outside the predominant group would most likely do better because it would be harder for that group to take advantage of him. An outsider would have more respect. Charlie liked the answer and I was offered the job. The Sun Bank Branch in Tamarac East had been a unit bank before and had been in operations for over 9 years. I was offered a substantial amount over my present salary, plus a car allowance and other benefits. There was only one hurdle I needed to jump and that was my loyalty to Manuel Fernandez. When someone helps you and treats you well, you should show thankfulness and appreciation. I went to Manuel and told him about the offer before I accepted it. He told me he also thought it was a good move and asked me to give him at least two weeks to find a replacement. I thanked him and did as he asked.

I was told by John Morris that they did not expect a rapid growth for this branch given that it was in a mature part of the city. He wanted me to maintain the current levels and to try to work with the current staff, that had been there for a while under the previous manager. The previous branch manager had been the unit president before the change in structure and was transferred to a lending officer position. I was not told the real reason he was transferred which I had to find out the hard way. After a few days on the job, I started to detect that the lady who was my assistant manager, was not fully cooperating with me. I sat with her and she told me that she was very upset that they transferred the other manager out, a move that she thought was unfair. I told her that I did not have anything to do with that decision and that I was there to maintain the branch and make it grow if I could. I detected that there was more to it than what she told me, so I started to ask questions and I got answers. Boy, did I get answers!

The real reason the previous manager was transferred was that even though he was married, he was having a romantic relationship with the assistant. This situation was causing all sorts of problems and potentially further problems. Banks were very cautious of their officers' reputation and any scandal could provoke loss of business and public confidence. The other problem was that some of the other staff members felt that the assistant manager, given her openly known relationship with the manager, was taking advantage of it and basically ran the branch firing or making it difficult for those who did not accept her unwarranted authority. Most banks and many other companies frown on married or engaged persons working together because it could lead to collusion, liability, and fraudulent activities. Many banks had policies that if two persons were working together and they got engaged, or married, one of them must be transferred to another unit that did not have joint activities. The matters complicate more when a supervisor and a subordinate are involved. This could lead to future sexual harassment claims when the relationship is terminated by the supervisor as the subordinate, who feels romantically betrayed, alleges that she or he was forced by the supervisor in a pro-quo claim.

This situation made my job harder because, my assistant, who is supposed to back me up and help me run the branch, was doing everything possible to make me fail. I spoke to my superiors who confirmed the events and they could not explain why I was not told. Their best reason was concerns with privacy. I needed to have my assistant in my corner if I were to succeed and I was not going to let this person ruin my chances. I had only three possible strategies to follow in order to correct the situation. One was to try to gain her support and confidence, the other was to terminate her, and the last one was to set performance standards for her that would lead to her resignation.

Termination without a solid documented trail, could bring added problem for me and the bank. Gaining her support would take longer than I had, so my only choice was to demand of her the performance needed and put strong pressure on her to do all the elements of her job well. To that effect I met with her and told her both verbally and in writing what I expected of her. She was visibly upset and told me that I was not been fair with her. I asked her to explain which areas were unfair and she could not because all of my requirements were the same other assistant managers in other branches were also asked to do. Her problem was that now she needed to work instead of just sitting there looking pretty. A few weeks later she resigned and I accepted her resignation.

My efforts in business development and community involvement paid off and made my branch grow more than the expectations, producing very healthy increases in my salary. The tide of banking consolidations continued to play havoc with banking careers. Sun Bank merged with another bank in Miami and formed one bank for both counties. This created changes and added more levels of management above me. It also changed who my supervisor was for the worse. My new supervisor was not familiar with me or with the work I had done and treated me with some disrespect. Some non-Hispanic bankers at the time and still today, do not treat Hispanic bankers with the same respect. Now that I had a solid history of excellent business development results and ample knowledge in lending and branch operations, I thought it was time to look for greener pastures.

Chapter Thirty Nine
Republic National Bank of Miami:
Years of growth and experience

While at Sun Bank my salary had increased by over 80% in four years which was excellent, but by 1980 my expenses also had increased with two of my children in Catholic elementary school and two in Catholic high school. The prospects for my career at Sun Bank were a little negative so I decided while on vacations that year to visit my old friend from the Cursillo meetings at Saint Michaels Catholic Church in Miami, Fred de la Mata, and see if he had a position for me at Republic National Bank of Miami.

This bank was founded by Ecuadorian capital and Cuban bankers with the strategy to serve the ever-growing Cuban population and to facilitate lending for many Cuban businessmen who were now in this country and after losing their businesses to Castro, were trying to establish themselves in Miami. The bank was very successful and was growing at a tremendous rate. The head of the bank was Mr. Aristides Sastre who was the main catalyst and visionary who made this success happen. Sastre had been a high-ranking banker in Cuba and knew most of the large business owners in Cuba. When these individuals came to him for a small loan to start their businesses in the U.S., Sastre took a chance with them and gave them the loan for which they were not qualified, but based upon their character and previous experience, Sastre trusted them and actually made, with his actions, many of the very large businesses that exist today.

Under Sastre, and supervising the International Department as well as the Branching department, was Fred de la Mata. Fred was also a banker from Cuba and had natural intelligence plus a deep knowledge of the market. I met with Fred one afternoon without prior notice, in his office on the fifth floor of the bank located on Flagler and Le Jeune Road in Miami. I told him about my experience and gave him a copy of my resume. He was impressed and told me if I would be interested in the position of branch manager at their new airport branch soon to open. I was very surprised that this offer was made so fast. I was used to a more bureaucratic behavior. I told him that I needed to think about it and talk to me wife and make a decision. The salary offered was about 20% more than my current salary plus a car and other benefits. It was a very tempting offer.

I went home and told Yolanda about it. Her first words were: "Are you sure you want to go back to Miami to a Cuban bank?" "Do you remember what happened before?" As always, she was right and I had thought about it, but I told her I did not think that this bank, which was very well established and profitable, would give me the same problems as the one before. We compared the two banks assessing the lack of future at Sun Bank compared to the prospect of utilizing my knowledge in a growing bank. We also compared salaries and benefits as well as the fact that at Republic I would not experience discrimination because I was Cuban. That analysis and knowing that there were some risks associated with the change; I went to see Fred de la Mata and accepted the offer. Fred took me up to the seventh floor to meet Mr. Aristides

Sastre. What a distinct pleasure that was. I found a man with no pretenses of greatness, simple, yet profound in his conversation. Sastre was a gentleman and his aura of visionary and innovator could be felt when you met him. He, of course, asked me about my father for whom he said had a lot of admiration.

Timing for this change could not have been better. The added salary and benefits were needed given the fact that in 1985 we had two children in Catholic elementary school (Robert and Joey), two in Catholic high school (Roland and Will), and two in college (Yolanda and Maria). In addition I was very active playing in different restaurants and parties. This school expense situation with all six in school continued until 1991 when we had two in elementary school and four in college. These were very difficult years where we experienced great budgetary pressures and required extreme teamwork between Yolanda and me to make ends meet every month. Credit cards were very helpful and the fact that our home's value had increased, allowed us to refinance our mortgage twice to pay down the credit card debt and lower our monthly debt service. We worked hard to increase our cash flow, control our extraordinary expenses, and maintain an excellent credit report.

The date was set and I submitted my resignation at Sun Bank. My supervisor accepted it without a word and asked me to leave right away. I was surprised because I had given the customary two weeks, but he told me to leave immediately. I did and I left without a trace of gratitude from the bank or respect from my supervisor after doing an excellent job. As banks get bigger they care less for their staff and act as if they do not appreciate what you do because as they say: "It is your job and you are lucky you have one." I called Fred and he told me to start right away. I then met with the head of Human Resources, Mrs. Ana Rios, who was very nice and helped me get all the paperwork done. When it came to the medical insurance I needed an exception because Sun Bank had cancelled mine and I could not wait the 30 days that Republic's policy required. Mrs. Rios told me that I needed to talk to Sastre about that. I went up to his office, he saw me right away and as I was asking his approval he picked up the phone and called Mrs. Rios and said: "Ana put Rolandito on the insurance right away." I thanked him for this. This action did so much for my commitment to this new job than even Sastre could imagine. In today's banking environment this would be impossible. No one today has that kind of authority in any bank.

The branch that I was hired to manage was a few months away from its opening and I found myself with little to do. Republic Bank was not as well organized as the other larger banks where I had worked. It had grown so fast, its procedures and policies were somewhat non-existent. I started to talk to other branch managers to learn from them the different procedure, etc. I was given a desk at the main office floor, so I could experience first-hand some of the procedures and had the chance to interact with customers. I also used my time to contact previous customers with the idea to bring them to Republic. All this activity did not fill my day and I was anxious. I was used to a multitasking and a busy workday. I then went to see Fred de la Mata and asked him if I could help him on a project or something to keep me busy. Fred thought for a moment and then said to me: "Ask Orlando Quintero, who was the VP and Cashier of the bank, to give you a copy of the overdraft list. I want you to analyze it and give me suggestions as to what we can do to minimize this activity." He then said that the examiners had criticized how this function was handled as well as the losses incurred from it. As I was leaving his office he asked me: "Rolandito, how do they handle overdraft in the other banks that you worked?" I turned to him and said: "We return the check." Fred smiled assuming that I was kidding. The funny part of this was that I was telling the truth.

At last I found something to keep me busy and where I could contribute. Mr. Quintero gave me the list and I went back to my desk to analyze it. This was a computer printout that measured over 4 inches in thickness, that included all the branches. I had never seen anything like it. There were accounts on the list showing over 300 days of overdraft. There were accounts with very large overdrafts. I thought something was wrong so I went back to Mr. Quintero and asked him about it. He explained that these accounts with 300 days were not really overdrafts. They were a product of the account closing the day before with an overdrawn balance. (Back then, banks always worked with numbers from the day before because posting of the transactions was only done at night after the banks closed. Today banks work with real-time activities).

The customer was contacted by the officer and asked to make a deposit to cover the overdraft before the deadline of 2:00 PM. If the customer made the deposit, the check would be paid and the account would be charged a fee for each check and interest in the amount borrowed for one day. If the customer did not make the deposit, the checks would be returned most of the time. There was little risk of losing using this method. That same day more checks would come in to the account, which would overdraw it, and the account would show overdrawn the next day. In effect the account showed overdraft for two consecutive days. The accounts with 300 days had done this 300 times.

This made it difficult to assess the risk of these accounts because the counter for the days showed so many days, but in reality that was not a good measure. What I did then was that I took all the accounts with overdrawn balances of $50,000 or more and went into the activity for each one of them to ascertain if it was a "true" overdraft of just a "day" overdraft. Once I had found those where there was more risk involved, I made an aging report showing the amounts that were overdrawn for 30, 60, 90, and 120 days. This report was very useful to Fred and Orlando to be able to contact the officers of these accounts and get their explanation of the problem. After several days large charge offs were made for those accounts considered to be a loss. Fred was happy and thanked me for the work done.

Several days passed and I was again looking for something to do and I went to Fred who told me to see Mr. Roberto Gonzalez-Blanco, Vice-Chairman in charge of investments, who had a project for me. I met with Roberto and he gave me the list of past due loans and asked me to do a similar analysis as I did for the overdrafts. This printout was more than 2 inches in thickness. This area had also been criticized by the examiners because the amounts were very high as well as the number of days past due. The results of my analysis was presented as an aging report and showed quite a few loans past due for many months and a very large amount of risk. Management was able to see clearly which loans needed attention and which officers needed to be contacted and asked to solve the situation or charge off the loan. This created a lot of turmoil given that it had not been done this way before. Many loans were charged off causing losses that were not anticipated.

The bank's Chairman of the Board was Dr. Luis J. Botifoll. He had been an attorney and newspaper editor in Cuba. Dr. Botifoll was a community leader and a high profile member of the Cuban American Foundation. Talking with him was like reading an encyclopedia. He had a fabulous memory and great personal anecdotes of his business dealings in Cuba, Central, and South America. He is by far the smartest person I have ever known, but at the same time he was very jovial and treated us as equals. For example, he did not have lunch at the executive suite, he came down to the employee cafeteria and sat with us every day. I feel extremely privileged to have known him.

In the meantime and because our never-ending need for extra income, I started playing and singing in different restaurants in Broward. I also played private parties. One of the restaurants that I played for several years was Costa Brava. This was a Spanish restaurant located on federal Highway where I played Thursdays, Fridays, and Saturdays. I had assembled a setup, which included bass pedals, guitar, rhythm machine and voice. I would play the bass with my feet, the guitar with my hands, the start/stop of the rhythm machine with one foot, I would sing, all at the same time. It took a lot of practice and independence of all four limbs to effectively do it. Back then we did not have the computerized music that we have today, so if I wanted to sound good, I had to do all that live.

The plans for my branch near the Miami International Airport were not progressing well. There were some problems with the lease of the building and also with the plans for the remodeling. Time continued to pass and I was in limbo. One day Roberto Gonzalez Blanco came to me and asked me if I could get from my previous banks a job description for the position of Credit Administrator. Roberto explained to me that the examiners had requested that the bank open a Credit Administration Department and he wanted to know what were the functions and job requirements. I assured him that I would be able to do it and I very quickly received, via fax, one from my good friend at Sun Bank who was in that position. I gave it to Roberto.

After a few days Roberto came to see me and told me that the management of the bank had decided to offer me the job of Credit Administrator. The job would give me $5,000 per year salary increase. I was taken aback because I was not trained for this job. I told Roberto that I was very thankful, but that I had never done this job, nor I had that much loan experience to do it. His words were: "Among all of us, you are the one who knows more about it, and we think you can learn it fast." There I was just a few months into my new job and I was already looking at the possibility of doing something new, helping the bank, but at the same time being thrown into what was the most difficult job of my career.

Chapter Forty
Republic National Bank of Miami:
Years of hard work and stress

The year was 1985 and Republic Bank was continuing its growth even though in 1982 a few of Republic's officers and a large customer left the bank to form Ocean Bank of Miami to compete head-to-head with Republic. The first few years Republic lost several large accounts and some other officers left for Ocean Bank. Republic's branch network was much larger than Ocean's and it was difficult for Ocean to compete, so Republic continued to grow and have financial success.

The bank examiners, The Office of the Comptroller of the Currency (OCC), were beginning to exert pressure on Republic for more controls given that the size of the bank warranted them. One of these requested changes was the creating of a Credit Administration Department, which would oversee the lending function and enforce the lending policies and procedures, including the loan operations and collateral controls among others. As the new Credit Administrator one of the first things I did was to review the bank's credit policy. When I was given it, I was surprised to see that it only consisted of five pages. I was used to the other banks' credit policies, which consisted of several volumes and hundreds of pages. My first recommendation to my direct supervisor, Fred de la

Mata, was to revise the policy and make it more complete. He agreed.

Another of the OCC's recommendations was to establish a Loan Review Department. This function reviews the loans and according to risks, classifies them into several categories. The higher the risks, the larger the loan loss reserves would be. This function requests from the officers handling these loans to come up with a remedial plan to declassify the loan. For this function the bank hired a former OCC examiner. This was a very smart move because this person had a lot of experience and would give credence to Republic's effort to correct deficiencies and would have an opportunity to create an easy channel of communications with the OCC. This officer had great experience and I was asked to work with him in the review of the credit policy.

We both worked hard in getting the credit policy up to par. Once we had finished it was presented to management and then to the board and it was approved. There were significant changes in it and right away it started to create a lot of protests among the loan officers. A lot of them blamed it on me because I was the enforcer, just like "kill the messenger." Many of these officers left the bank and went to work at Ocean Bank where the policies resembled those previously used at Republic. I am not going to judge some of these officers, but the reason for their departure was for the most part that they could no longer do as they pleased and maybe could no longer do some shady deals with the customers. In any event we started calling Ocean Bank as "Hermanos al Rescate" (Brothers to the Rescue). Brothers to the Rescue was an excellent organization that flew in the Florida strays trying to alert the Coast Guard of "balseros" (rafters) so they could be rescued. Cubans have the tendency of using humor even if it means an apparent disrespect. Brothers to the Rescue was later attacked by Castro's fighter jets and two of the three civilian planes in international waters were shot down and four crew members died while the Clinton Administration did nothing.

The new credit policy did its job in identifying loans that were actual losses that had been hidden for years. The Credit Review Department identified and charged off over $20 million in bad loans between the years 1985 and 1986. Another function that was started was the Credit Analysis Department whose responsibility was to analyze new and current loans and give an opinion as to risk. I started this department and the standards were set and the procedures established. The area of loan documentation was also in need of repair. We created a section with analysts to review the documentation of every new or renewed loan before it was booked. I was appointed secretary to the loan committees and I was given the charge to review that the loans were presented within the parameters of the policy and that the documentation was correct.

The activities done prior to the loan committee gave me the greatest stress and at the end resulted in many officers resenting my comments and observations when they presented a loan for approval. I was like the "devil's advocate," but many of the officers took it as a personal attack. Given that I take responsibilities seriously I tried to do this job as well as possible and many times, I now recognize, took matters to unnecessary extremes. Knowing how important it is to make sound and policy-compliant loans, I was at times abrupt and right out nasty with the officer presenting. I regret that and I apologize to those who I offended.

As if I did not have enough stress already, one day Fred de la Mata asked me to move my office to the Bird Road branch because the branch manager had left for Ocean Bank and he needed someone there to try to retain employees and customers. He thought that I could do both jobs from there for a few months. I agreed and I took my secretary with me so she could help me cope with the situation. I found that the employees were very confused. Some had left already with the manager, who by the way was and is a good friend of mine, some of the other employees acted like they were also leaving given the way they talked to customers. These "spies" were left behind to make contact with the customers and tell them to go to Ocean. I respectfully told this group to go now. I was working with a skeleton crew and started to hire new employees to cover the empty positions. I also spoke to all the customers that came in trying to retain them and got a list of the largest customers and tried to visit them. This last group had almost all gone to Ocean. One of the tellers came to me because she had been offered a job at Ocean and wanted to know what were her chances at Republic, because she needed to progress and wanted to expand her career, I spoke to Human Resources and got her a small raise and told her that I would do everything in my power to help her. There were a few others who I retained.

After a few months we found a branch manager and I was able to go back to my job fulltime, but I had a problem. My secretary decided that she would rather stay at the branch because she liked the customer contact better than working with reports and papers all day. I used to tease her telling her that the reason she left me was because the new branch manager was younger and handsomer than me. There I was without a secretary, and then I remembered that teller that had desires to progress and do more. I spoke to her about the job and she accepted it with the condition that I had her trained well. This turned out to be one of my most brilliant moves. This new secretary learned very fast and moved to the ranks so fast that today she is a Vice President and lender for a large bank and worked her way through school and obtained an MBA.

Back in Credit Administration the person that was the supervisor for the loan operations area had been there for decades and she was used to doing things as they always did. One of the problem areas was officers sending loans to be booked above their lending limits. I needed to stop that practice and proceeded to instruct this supervisor to make sure that she did not book any loan that was outside the limits. One day she came to me with a very sarcastic smile on her face and told me that she had a line of credit renewal that was presented by an officer, which was above that officer's lending limit. She wanted my opinion as to what to do because that officer was no other than Mr. Sastre the president of the bank. I knew she was trying to test me with this difficult issue, but I told her to give me the papers and that I would take care of it for her. I went to the seventh floor to talk to Mr. Sastre and he received me right away as he always did. I told him that this line was over his limit and that I was going to book it, but I wanted his permission to take it to the loan committee to ratify it, given that it was above his limit. This was the first time that anybody had stopped one of Mr. Sastre's transactions and I was very apprehensive as to what he would say.

Sastre looked at me and with a blank facial expression told me to leave it with him that he would take care of it. I left his office thinking that maybe my days left at Republic were short. The next Loan Committee, Mr. Sastre started the meeting by saying: "I need for you to approve the renewal of this line of credit given that Rolandito would not book it without the committee's approval." Of course that is not what I said, but I did not correct him. All eyes were on me and I felt like one inch tall. To this day I do not know if Mr. Sastre was actually upset with me or he was testing me. I do not know if he wanted to embarrass me or actually send a message to all the others that if Rolandito could stop one of his loans, he could stop any of yours. Knowing what I know now of Mr. Sastre, I am almost sure he did it to help me and the bank.

In the meantime the management of the bank decided to create a position of Chief Credit Officer and I was bypassed, surely because of my newly created fame, and named the person in charge of Loan Review, who was a former OCC examiner, who now became my new supervisor. I first resented it, but got used to it. I had a really good job now making around $70,000 per year and I decided to make every effort to work well with my new boss. Also I had been approved to attend the University of Miami Executive Master in Business Administration (MBA). This was a great benefit because the bank offered to pay 100% of it as long as I stayed one year after graduation.

This program was designed for people that had fulltime jobs. It was held on Saturdays all day for 28 straight months. I applied for it because it did not require that the student have a Bachelor's Degree. The requirements were: 10 years or more in a management position, successfully passing the GMAT exam, having your employer sponsor you, and passing an interview with the Dean. I successfully complied with all of these and was accepted to start in January 1988.

That year I also started to play at a Broward County restaurant called Don Arturo located near Davie Boulevard in Fort Lauderdale. I played in this Cuban restaurant Fridays and Saturdays. One day the owners Pedro Gonzalez and his wife asked to bring two more musicians for a special Valentine's party that they had. They wanted to make the music more danceable. I spoke to my good friend and fellow banker Felix (Felito) Calderin who played the drums and my classmate from my school in Cuba Armandito Romeu to play the vibraphone and keyboards. We did a couple of rehearsals in Felito's home and we were ready. Armandito is an accomplished musician who comes from a family of famous and well-known Cuban musicians. These two pieces gave the group a real great sound and both were able to follow me without any trouble. The owners liked us so much that they decided to hire us for both days permanently, well permanently for musicians means as long as the owners want.

With the practice of two days per week playing we became even better. I had an extensive repertoire and both my fellow musicians were able to follow me many times without any rehearsal. The last set of Friday, we started using for rehearsing new songs. We would play Cuban, Spanish, Latin American, American and even Italian songs. The public really liked us and we were there for over one year. The restaurant would pay us $50.00 each day a piece and we then split the tips three ways. Then the restaurant was sold to a Cuban family that did not want us there and without notice they literally kicked us out. Faced with that we decided to present a show in a small theatre in Calle 8 to start promoting our group for parties, weddings, etc. We named the group "Los Juniors" because all of us had the same first name as our fathers. We were fairly successful and played in a few places. Then we added a conga player, then a female singer, and later a sax player. A few months later another female singer and we had formed a very respectable band.

The turmoil continued at Republic Bank where I was always the bad guy while my boss was the good guy even though it was he who told me what to do. One day my boss accompanied by the principal owner of the bank came into my office on the second floor, closed the door, and said that they needed to talk to me. Of course I thought it was all over for me at Republic, but I tried to remain calm and sat down as well. The principal owner of the bank told me: "Rolando, everybody is saying that you are a Son-of-a-Bitch." I told him that my mother did not have any fault for what I had done. The principal owner then said: "No, it is okay. The moment they stop saying that, I will fire you." This conversation gave me even more stress. I knew I needed to soften my approach if I would ever have a chance for a promotion, but then I was told by the "Owner of the ponies." (This is a Cuban expression, "El dueño de los Caballitos" that we use to signify the top decision maker) that I must continue to be the bad guy.

To this day there are bankers that speak ill of me and at times have blocked my hiring at other banks. I understand their feelings and I forgive them in the hope that they do the same for me. I know that many of them learned a lot from these situations and many became better lending officers under the pressures that I put them through. I would like to think that my efforts made Republic Bank a better bank even though many loans were still approved as exceptions to the policy and after my negative comments. There were some events that took place in 1987 that put Republic Bank in a bad light. The bank was in the news for a long time and these events resulted that in 1988 Fred de la Mata left the bank and some other officers did as well. I have chosen not to comment on these events because they are public record and I do not want for my comments to hurt those involved more than they have already suffered. The bank was restructured and the new president was Mr. Oscar Bustillo, who had been in charge of the International Department.

I continued in my position for a while and the bank suffered the loss of some customers, but was still very profitable. The job of Credit Administrator was not very attractive to me and I was getting tired of the negative image. I devised a plan for me to go back to what I was good at, business development and utilizing all that I had learned at the MBA program that I completed in May 1990. The plan was to hire a new Credit Administrator and I would start a new position called Business Development Officer (BDO). As BDO I would go after the large Hispanic businesses that were not currently banking with Republic and try to get them to switch banks. Bustillo liked the idea and we hired the new person and after a month or so I started my new job. I continued to report to the head of credit. I started with the list of the Largest Hispanic Businesses, selected those in South Florida, deleted those we already had, and constructed a prospects list.

I started making appointments to visit these businesses and was able to meet a few of them. I sent letters to the others which were followed up by more phone calls to get an appointment. I organized a cocktail party at our seventh floor reception area and invited all of them. Many came and I had the help of the senior officers of the bank that evening in order to impress upon my prospects that they would deal with the decision makers. I was able to convince a few to apply for loans and lines, which was the first step needed to make the switch. When I went to Loan Committee to get these loans approved I found that several of the members of the committee were very negative to my presentations and they were getting even with me for the hard time I had given them in the past. It was a hard road, but I was able to approve two loans. This was not a good beginning, but I knew that, given time, I would succeed.

In 1989 when our youngest child was 10, Yolanda decided to go back to work. First she took computer courses so she could be ready for the workforce and then procured a part time job with a doctor in Fort Lauderdale. She was handling medical insurance claims and she worked until 2:00 PM, at which time she had to pick up the two youngest at the elementary school, which was near the doctor's office. It worked out great and helped the cash flow of our family without losing the attention that children needed from their parents. Yolanda worked there until 2003.

During that time I started to teach at the University of Miami Koubek Center where they had business and banking classes in Spanish for foreign students from Latin America that wanted to learn how things were done in the U.S. I was teaching Marketing, Money and Banking and Principles of Banking. This was a great part-time job and also gave me practice in teaching in Spanish. As mentioned before, at that time we had two in college, two in high school, and two in elementary school. The tuition, books, uniforms, dorm fees, meals, gas, car insurance, and incidentals was a large nut to crack every month. I was lucky that I had the energy and the opportunity to do all this to help our children get a good education.

After a few months, the bank made a restructure and I was asked to be the head of the Consumer Lending area. Reporting to my same boss. The area consisted of Installment Lending, Small Business Administration (SBA) Lending, Credit Cards, Mortgages Lending, Auto Lending, Collections, and Consumer Loan Operations. This was an important part of the bank and I was happy to be able to contribute given the weak results of my business development efforts. My first crisis came when the head of the Residential Mortgage department left the bank and I was asked to go there and run it while I found a replacement. Frankly I had very little experience in this product and I had a hard time supervising it for a few months. Fortunately I found a great replacement. This lady had lots of experience and was perfect for the job. Throughout the interview process we spoke only English. She was blonde with green eyes and had an American last name. I thought she was not Cuban because that question cannot be asked. It really did not matter because she had the best qualifications. Later I found out she was 100% Cuban.

Bustillo and my boss called me for a meeting at Bustillo's office. I had a bad feeling about it and I was right. Bustillo had made some restructuring and had created a new Retail Division, which would include all the branches and all the consumer credit products, and he wanted me to be a regional manager within that division. I would supervise the Main Region, which included the main branch, and the consumer lending area that I already headed. The other three regions would be only composed of branches and were named; North, Central, and South. All four regional managers would report to the person selected by Bustillo for this job. Frankly I thought I was better qualified for it than he was, but my bad reputation and the fact that Bustillo and him were good friends, took away from me this opportunity. I did not dislike my new boss, but found him incompetent, inexperienced, and what was worse, rude.

Of course I accepted the change because it came with more salary and as I saw it with a lot of responsibility and chances to do a good job. After I finished my meeting with Bustillo and my old boss, I came down to the sixth floor to my new boss's office. I greeted him and asked if I could close his door. After the door was closed I said to him: "I just heard that you are my new boss and I want to tell you that you can count on my support and hard work, but I would like to ask you a favor." He said to go ahead and I told him that if he ever had to reprimand me, I would like for him to do it behind closed doors and not in front of others. He told me: "I have never done that." I said: "Yes, you have." Then he said: "I know who I can do it to and who I cannot do it to." I said to him: "Please put me in the list of those you do not do it to." Then I left. Not what you call a great beginning, but I needed to get that out of my system.

The year was 1992 and I began to organize my Region better. I started to have weekly meetings with the department heads in order to establish excellent teamwork among all of them. The Main Branch was larger in deposits than all the other branches put together so my region held more than half of the bank's deposits. All the consumer loan departments plus the SBA were all approved and operated centrally by my region and the collections department had many experienced collectors.

In 1992 both of our daughters graduated from college. Yolanda with Doctorate in Veterinary Medicine and Maria with a Master in Education. We still had Joey in elementary, Robert in high school, and Roland and Will in college. That year I also started to teach at Miami Dade College in the Banking program in addition to teaching at the University of Miami and playing with my band. Yolanda, my wife, continued with her job at the doctor's office as well. In 1993 our son Roland graduated with a bachelor in Theatre and English and in 1994 our son Will graduated with a bachelors in Wild Life Ecology.

In 1995 I stopped teaching at the University of Miami, but continued with Miami Dade College and the band. Teaching at Miami Dade College was part of my future plans. I wanted to teach after my retirement from banking. The reason was that, number one; I needed to work until the end of my life because I had not accumulated enough retirement funds to stop working and the social security retirement amount would not be sufficient to maintain our standard of living. Number two; banking was changing and my future did not look so bright due to my age. Number three; I really like teaching and this is a profession where being old is not a problem. Lessons to be learned from my experience; save money for your retirement and work at something you really like.

Chapter Forty One
Republic National Bank of Miami:
Time for a change

My relationship with the boss was very stressful mainly because he did not want to make any decisions and everything was left pending. He told me one day that his method consisted of letting things sit unresolved because 85 % of them would not be requested again, so he would only have to deal with the 15% that insisted. Not what you call a model management style. He also did not like to receive too many memos. We did not have emails back then so most of the communications was done via memos. He came to my office one day and told me that I wrote too many memos and that he did not want to be copied on them. So I said: "How do I keep you informed?" He told me to go to his office and tell him in person when something was important. The problem was that when I went to see him, he was either not there or he told me he was busy to come back later. This style of management was very difficult for me to work under. I am a man of action and I am always looking for better ways to do things. I am also a detailed person who does not like to do things incomplete.

I decided that I would get a copy of the item in question, send it interoffice, and stick a note to it that says "I need to see you on this." I did that but he would return it back to me interoffice with his writing in red saying "Let's discuss."

Once I got it, I would put it in one of my drawers to wait his follow-up that never came. My region and my departments were doing great. I promoted my secretary to lending officer and put her in charge of the SBA loans. She became really good at that and was a hard worker, very loyal, and got along well with all the others.

I had been at Republic for over 13 years and even though I had progressed in my career and in my salary, Republic had been very hard work and a lot of stress. Now it was worse than ever because of my boss. I counted the time I worked for him the same way the Jewish people counted their time in the desert. I worked for him 40 months! There were also rumors that they were going to sell the bank. At this time there were many big banks coming down to Florida and buying smaller banks. Republic was a good target for an out of state bank to obtain instant market ratio. I was not looking for a job, but I was constantly being called by different headhunters and also by one of the directors of another Cuban bank in Hialeah called Ready State Bank.

I met with Ready State Bank officials and waited almost 30 days with no response. A headhunter called me about a position at a fairly new local bank called Hamilton Bank and I went for an interview with its chairman. He liked me and offered me a job as Division Manager making about 10% more and a lot of benefits. Given my discontent at Republic and the prospects of a takeover by another bank, I made the decision to go to Hamilton Bank. This turned out to be the wrong decision. I should have stayed at Republic and then waited to see what happened, but the thought of not having a job scared me. It is easier to be a "Monday morning quarterback." When the director of Ready State Bank found out that I was going to Hamilton Bank, he called me and offered me a job. I told him no because I had already committed to Hamilton Bank. He told me that I made the wrong decision and that I was not going to last there. He also said to call him if I ever wanted to make the change.

The year was 1996 and our son Robert graduated from high school in 1995 and had started college. Our son Will entered the U.S. Air force as a Second Lieutenant in 1994 after successfully completing the ROTC program. Our son Will was also the first to get married in 1994 to our daughter in law Stephanie Morris. Our budget was a little less demanding those days. This was good given what was coming in the near future. To add to the stress, my dear mother had died in December 3, 1995 after a few years of illness. Losing my mother was hard for me, but in a way I was glad because of her condition. My father was devastated. He had been the primary caretaker during her illness and that year on December 18, they were to celebrate their 60th wedding anniversary.

My father spent the days after my mother's death alone in his apartment in Hialeah. My sisters and I visited him as much as we could. In one of those visits that I made I found him still in his pajamas and unshaved even though it was late afternoon. He looked very sad and with little desire to converse. I was quite worried about his condition and then I asked him a blunt question: "Dad do you want to die too?" He answered no and looked at me with a look, which was a combination of surprise and sadness. I told him that he needed to look for something to keep him busy, because if he stayed all day by himself and in pajamas, the sadness would kill him. Why don't you find a job? I said. He said: "Me at my age, who would give me a job. He was 79 and in good health of body and mind at the time.

I thought for a minute then I told him that he needed to go see his good friend Luis Sabines because Sabines knew everybody in Miami and he would find him a job. Sabines was the founder and president of the largest Latin Chamber of Commerce in Miami and in the past my father had worked in their events. I told him: "Tomorrow morning you get up early, shave, and wear one of those very expensive suits that you have with one really good tie, drive down to Miami, and visit Luis Sabines in the Chamber located on Flagler Street. He is your good friend and he will help you."

My father looked at me with the Ringling's sad clown face that he often used. He would use this face whenever he needed to do something he did not want to do. My sisters and I were very familiar with this face which was manufactured by him to solicit pity. I acted as if the face was not there and said: "What do think of that idea?" He reluctantly agreed and did as I proposed. Luis Sabínes was a friend of friends and had a tremendous admiration for my father as many of their generation did. When my father asked him to help him get a job, Sabines paused for a few seconds then said: "Rolando, ya está resuelto! (I have the solution!) Mañana empiezas a trabajar aquí comigo (Tomorrow you start to work here with me)" Shaken by this great man's friendship and respect my father asked him what was he going to do. Sabínes said for him to be there tomorrow and then he will see.

As soon as he could, my father called me to tell me. I congratulated him, but he was worried because he did not know what he was going to do. My father had a great sense of responsibility and professionalism in all he did and always gave 100% to his work. The next day came and my father was there early. He was always early to every event in his life. He had learned this from his days in the theatre. In those days if a play was supposed to start at 8:00 PM, it started at 8:00 PM and you had to be ready.

Sabínes had a program with federal funds to employ the elderly and my father was now the new member of this group of about six other "third age" persons. He sat behind a desk and all day he awaited to be given something to do. The end of the workday came and he had not done anything all day. He called me when he got home and told me he was going to quit because he was not going to be paid for doing nothing. He said he had never done that. I told him not worry that it was just the first day and that things would change with time. Besides, I told him that he could not do that to Sabínes after he had given him that opportunity. The next day after work, he called me to tell me that he had worked very hard that day because he had sent 5 faxes. My father would always use humor to make things better for him. My father was there for 3 years and Sabínes also used him to entertain foreign dignitaries from Latin American countries with his monologues and jokes. Sabínes helped my father live many more years by his friendship and love. Sabínes was a true friend.

I resigned at Republic. This was very hard to do because after 13 years one creates a lot of relationships that will be missed, and starting again at another bank was not what I wanted to do at this stage of my life and career. This decision started the decline of my banking career. After just over a year, I left Hamilton due to differences of opinion with the chairman. I contacted the director at Ready State Bank and he offered me a job of Lending Officer with a substantial reduction in salary. I accepted it because I had a bad feeling about Hamilton Bank. Hamilton Bank was closed by the government a few years later and its chairman and other officers were sentenced to jail. I have chosen not to discuss the details of this situation because I do not want to hurt those involved who have suffered enough already.

In 1997 our son Joey started college. I was still teaching at Miami Dade College and playing with my band. While at Hamilton we had moved to our new home in Pembroke Pines after 28 years living in the same house in Plantation. The mortgage payment was much higher, but we had a larger home in a much better area where we thought the value would increase rapidly. The larger mortgage payment made difficult for our budget given that I was making less money. My total earnings from 1996 to 1997 were reduced by 14%.

In 1998 our son Will finished his Master in Information Technology while serving in the U.S. Air Force as a pilot.

My job at Ready State Bank was to bring commercial loans and accounts to the bank. I did not have any administrative duties. There were many officers doing the same at the bank and many of them were members of the loan committee, which had to approve all the requests. I was not a member. I started to bring numerous loan requests to the committee and most of them were denied. The director who recruited me told me that I had brought more requests than most of the other loan officers. Then I put two and two together and understood why my requests were denied because of professional jealousy. Out of over $25 million dollar in requests, the committee had only approved $5 million. After just five months there, one day the president of the bank, who was also a loan officer with production responsibilities, came to my office and fired me. He told me that I was supposed to have five million in closed loans and I only had 3.5 million. I told him two things: I was never given a quota and I had $5 million approved and the rest of it was ready to be closed. I understood why I was fired. The president and other senior officers saw in me too much competition and the possibility, given my administration experience, that I would take their jobs. When I called the director that for years had been after me, he did not help and just said that the decision was made.

They offered me 30 days paid to help me find another job, but I told them that I did not want to stay there one more minute and I left. Not a very smart thing to do, but I let my pride and temper get the best of me. I was now unemployed for the first time in my marriage. The year 1998 was a very active year for bank mergers and acquisitions hence there were many middle management jobs that were eliminated and none of the banks were hiring. I tried for almost a month and I did not find a banking job, I even started to apply for out of the state jobs, but could not get one either. I was getting really worried as our small savings started to deplete. Yolanda and I went into a budget crisis mode and I added more classes to my schedule at Miami Dade College and I tried to increase the activity in my band. I thought of selling our new home and look for something smaller.

Chapter Forty Two
Urbieta Enterprises:
It is good to have friends

The stress level was as high as it has been since the days leading to our departure from Cuba in 1962. I questioned whether I should continue my banking career or find another one, but what could I do? Both Yolanda and I prayed for a solution and Yolanda always helped me with her hope and faith when I was ready to give it up. I talked to everyone and asked everyone I met to help me get a job, but nothing seemed to work. My self esteem and confidence was at the bottom of the ocean. It reminds me of my times in basic training in the army when our drill sergeant used to say: "You know what you are? You are lower than the whales' (@@@@@) excrement."

When I was at Sun Bank back in 1981 I had met a young man who together with his father were running a couple of Amoco gas stations. One in Miami Beach and the other one in Tamarac, very close to my branch in Commercial Blvd. One day this young entrepreneur, who had become a friend came to see me and asked for a small loan to buy another gas station in Margate Florida. I trusted him and approved this small loan under my lending authority. This hard working family made the new station a success in no time and then came to request funding for another station. We had the opportunity to finance their initial growth.

When I left Sun Bank and came to Republic Bank I arranged a meeting with the head of our Commercial Real Estate Department because Urbieta Enterprises, that was the name of my friend's business, wanted financing for their next phase which was the acquisition of the real estate at each station and the building of de novo ones. The head of this department made a very bad decision, denied the request. I then spoke to a friend I had at Ocean Bank who had worked at Republic before and referred the Urbietas to him. Ocean Bank was able to approve the request and helped Urbieta Enterprises to be among the largest Hispanic companies in the U.S. today.

Learning what had happened to me at Ready State Bank, both Urbieta brothers asked me out to lunch one day. They had a proposition for me. They wanted me to be their CFO and help them in the office and with several departments. At first I thought they just wanted to help me, but as they spoke, I realized that I could be of help to them as well. It was a good alternative and they paid me as much as they could at the time. This pay was about 50% of what I was making at the last bank, but that was immaterial because I did not have a bank job anymore and this opportunity was great for me. I will be forever grateful to them.

This job came just in time because in 1999 our son Joey graduated from Broward College where he had a two-year full scholarship and was accepted to the University of California Berkeley to study physics. We were able to help him cover the costs and things were more stable as far as the budget was concerned. I continued to teach at Miami Dade College and play with my band, and Yolanda continued to work for the doctor. God heard Yolanda's prayers and provided for what we needed.

The job at Urbieta was totally different than the one at the bank and it took me a while to get used to it. I had some knowledge of the business because of my involvement with them as customers, but there was a lot more that I did not know. The oldest brother, who was an engineer for Florida Power and Light Company, had decided several years before to join the family business. He was a great complement to the younger brother and they made a wonderful team. I took over some of the responsibilities of the older brother and I came up with ideas and methods to better organize them and improve them. I felt that I was making a contribution to their operations and they continued to grow and expand their footprint.

Their central office was located in Tamarac and for convenience I started to look for a nearby bank where I could do my personal banking. I remembered that my good friend and two times boss, Manuel Fernandez, was the president of Security Bank in North Lauderdale. I went there and opened two personal accounts. I would go every week to deposit my payroll and took the opportunity to talk to Manuel about the "good old days."

On one such day Manuel told me that he had a proposition for me. He was expanding the branch network and he wanted to know if I would be interested in the job of Branch Administrator. I thought I was through with banking, but this proposition awakened my love for the profession. The pay would be about the same, but with some additional benefits. The only problem was my desire not to offend or hurt my good friends the Urbietas. I talked to them and told them about this opportunity. They were very gracious and understood my decision to come back to banking. I hope that my short stay with Urbieta Enterprises contributed a little to their success in the subsequent years. We are still friends to this day and many times I have been able to play with my band in their company Holiday parties.

Chapter Forty Three
Back to Banking

I was now working at Security Bank for Manuel Fernandez Grande for the third time in my banking career. Manuel, as mentioned before, was a wonderful manager and one of the smartest bankers I have met. The bank was very well organized and my job was to supervise the seven branches and the mortgage department. Security Bank was a small community bank whose principal stockholder was a family from Mexico who were good friends of Manuel's. Many of the supervisors, branch managers, and staff had worked for Manuel at Landmark Bank or Southeast Bank. This made it easier for me because I knew many of them.

My desk, I did not have an office at first, was in the lobby of the main branch located in North Lauderdale, from there I would visit the branches as much as I could to provide support and guidance. There was one branch in Miami, three in Broward County, and three in Palm Beach County. The territory was quite large and I did a lot of driving, but I was happy to be back to banking. My time at Security was short, not quite a year, but I truly enjoyed it.

One day I got a call from a banker with whom I worked at Republic Bank, Ana Maria Perez, who was now working as a Branch Manager at Bank Atlantic. Ana Maria told me that her bank was looking for a Market Manager for the two of the branches located in Northeast Miami Dade. I told her that I was very happy where I was, but when she told me what the starting salary was, my interest was awakened. At Security Bank my salary was about two-thirds of what I was making in Ready State Bank and since then I had to increase my teaching and music activities in order to make ends meet. This possible change could do two things for me: first it would increase my salary and second it would place me in a much larger bank, where maybe I would re-start my career. I told my good friend Ana Maria that I would pursue it.

The next day I received a call from Mrs. Marta Armas, who was one of the Regional Managers for Bank Atlantic, to set up a meeting. I was to meet with her first and then with the president for Miami Dade County Jose Valle. I came down to their office and met with them and they made me the offer to be the Market Manager for the Aventura and Hallandale branches. I then went to Manuel and told him about the offer. Manuel told me to accept it and wished me luck. I accepted the offer and started at Bank Atlantic. My office was in the Aventura Branch in an out-parcel in Biscayne Boulevard at Lowman's Plaza. My new boss, Marta Armas, turned out to be one of the best bosses I have ever had. She was so supportive and always respected my experience and me, and was always ready to praise me when I reached the sales goals.

Our family continued to grow with the arrival of our first grandchild. Grace Madeleine Hennekens was born in April 2001. I worked at Bank Atlantic for over four years and I was able to increase my salary close to the levels I had in 1997. Bank Atlantic had a very good production incentive plan and I was able to show a high level of productivity. During the last two years there (2003 and 2004) the bank suffered a model change. The bank copied and adopted a model created by Commerce Bank in Pennsylvania called the "Most Convenient Bank." Bank of Commerce was America's Most Convenient Bank and Bank Atlantic was Florida's Most Convenient Bank. The business model consisted in opening the branches 7 days a week and all kinds of hours. It also included totally free checking accounts and many other free services. Bank Atlantic was heavily into residential mortgages and during those years we were experiencing the boom. Bank Atlantic could afford to lose its shirt by offering free everything and 7-day banking because they were making lots of money in the mortgages.

From the beginning of this business model, I thought it was not a good idea. Banks and all businesses must have different sources of income and service charge income was and still is a very important source. Opening 7-days was another bad idea because it created additional payroll expenses and mostly produced tiny low balance accounts and lots of low margin branch activity. Who would go to a bank on a Sunday? Not the wealthy individual to open a large certificate account, not the large business to open a profitable checking account, but the low balance customers who worked so hard during the week in two or three jobs.

Bank of Commerce sued Bank Atlantic on the basis that Bank Atlantic had copied their model. Bank of Commerce lost because the courts determine that you could not "copyright" an idea or a business model. Bank of Commerce then started to buy banks in South Florida to compete head-to-head with Bank Atlantic. Bank Atlantic was never the same after that and I started to feel that I needed a change. Bank of Commerce was later acquired by Toronto Dominion Bank, better known as TD Bank. TD Bank has maintained some of the model, but with a lot of adjustments.

During those days and because of the boom (bubble), I used to get several phone calls per week from recruiters (A/K/A Head Hunters) offering me positions at others banks. For years I told them that I was happy at Bank Atlantic, but after the business model change, I was more receptive and one of those calls was for a position at Bank United for their Aventura Branch. I did a little research on Bank United and found it to be attractive at the time. It was a local bank at the time being run by Ramiro Ortiz with whom I had worked at Landmark Bank. I went for several interviews and I was offered the position of VP and Bank Manager of the Aventura Branch. I went to lunch with Marta Armas, my boss, and when I told her I was leaving, we both got teary eyed. We had established a great friendship that has lasted to the present.

The year was 2004 and several changes had occurred that year. I started at Bank United, Yolanda started to work at Navix Imaging after 14 years working with the gastroenterologist in Fort Lauderdale, I stopped my teaching part time at Miami Dade College and The Center for Financial Training, and I applied and was accepted to Nova Southeastern University's Doctor in Business Administration program. You can say that 2004 was a big year of change for us. The added salary and benefits at Bank United allowed me to make these changes. The only part time job that I kept was the band. The question might be: Why make so many changes at a time? There were many reasons. Stay tuned.

Chapter Forty Four
Retirement Planning

My banking career has been very rewarding. I had my excellent years, years of growth and learning, years of hard unappreciated work, years of decline, and years in dead end jobs. Overall I was able to support my family and give our children a solid education. Also I was able to go to college and get a Masters degree. Since 1998 to 2004 my career was in a flat line as far as promotions and added administrative responsibilities. From 2000 to 2004 I was a branch manager for Bank Atlantic, then I became a branch manager in Bank United with very little chances of promotions. Banking had changed from having many administrative and executive positions available for experienced bankers, to having mostly "sales" jobs where you can only make more money by selling more. It turned from how much you knew about banking and retaining and servicing your customers, to how much new business you could bring.

In August 2005 our second grandchild was born, Isabella Ashley Ochoa. In February 2007 our third grandchild was born William James Ochoa and in May 2007 our fourth, Thomas (TJ) Dee Woods was born.

Banking, as most other business in the world, had become a jungle where each enterprise must do better this year than the last. A lot of the blame, in my opinion goes to Wall Street and the stock analysts, given that most large enterprises are public companies. If your company or bank made a net profit after taxes of $10 Million dollars one year, but only made $9 Million dollars the following year, the analysts consider you sort of a failure and the price of your stock goes down as well as the value of the company. This, in my opinion, is utter nonsense. This sick mentality puts the pressure on the leadership of these companies to outperform themselves every month, every quarter, and every year. This pressure trickles down to every department head, every branch manager, every employee. I remember having a banner month where I blew my goals out of the water, but then had a very slow starting next month and receiving a lot of pressure from the powers that be.

Bank Atlantic was that way and Bank United was the same. I was fortunate to meet most of my goals, but that pressure was making me literally sick. I was not enjoying my work and I was not able to help my employees and customers because of the lack of authority given to me. Every decision needed somebody else's approval. I saw myself not as banker, but a salesman. Selling is good as a complement of your professional and administrative performance. When selling became the only thing I did, I knew that my days as a banker were short.

Because we made the decision to have six children, for which we are very happy, because we had chosen to give them a Catholic education, and because we had insisted that all of them get a college degree, our retirement funds were not going to be enough once we retired. We had a few dollars in some IRAs and the social security for both of us, but these were not enough to maintain the standard of living that we wanted. I knew that I would have to work until I die.

Let me make a point about social security. First this is not "an entitlement," as many dishonest politicians and media mouth-pieces call it. The funds that people in social security get, are their own funds that they are getting back as a benefit that comes from working hard all their lives and "contributing" to this fund so when they retire they will get it back, plus interest. Social security taxes were and are mandatory and are paid from earnings. Your monthly "return" (Not benefit, not entitlement) should depend on how much you have contributed in your work life. We know that there are some people who get social security payments who did not contribute to the fund, and/or never worked a day in their lives. For this last group, these payments are an entitlement and in my opinion should not come from the social security funds. We know that our "esteemed" and "honest" politicians have changed many of the original rules and have used the fund to cover some of the other shortages due to their incompetency and pork-barrel activities.

The reality for me was that I was not going to last very long as a banker. First, because I did not like what I was doing and it was making me sick, and also because I knew that an older banker working for a large bank had little future. Young inexperienced "bankers" are better suited to be good salesmen. They do not know any better so they follow new trends and new business models without questions. So I knew I had to find another career where I could work until I die. Because I had been teaching for over 20 years and because I really liked to do it, I decided that teaching would be my new career. Having a Master's degree qualifies you to teach in most places, but the trend started to be that in order to assure you of a full time teaching position in a college or university, you needed a doctorate degree. That was the reason I started at Nova University, which at the time was the only university I could find where I could get a doctorate degree while still working full time. I started in August 2004.

I had to stop my part-time teaching jobs at Miami Dade College and The Center for Financial Training and I also cut down a little bit on the band's activities in order to have sufficient time to devote to my classes and studies. I was 61 years old when I started and at that age your brain does not retain as much as if you were in your late twenties which is when you are supposed to do your doctorate. My classmates were all much younger than me and many of my professors as well, but I was determined to do it. Many people asked me why I was doing such a thing and I told them that that was my retirement plan. In 2006 our daughter Maria got married to Thomas Woods and they were living in New Orleans.

During the first years at Nova University I did well and was passing all my classes mostly with As and a couple of Bs. I was still working at Bank United when the bubble burst in the mortgage industry and produced a near collapse of our financial system. I am not going to explain what happened here, but I recommend that you watch a documentary entitled "Inside Job" which in my opinion explains this situation quite well and places the blame where it belongs on the greed of those involved. Bank United was hit pretty badly. Most of our lending was residential mortgages and we had entered into those infamous negative amortization loans. What are those you ask? Very simply, the monthly payment from the customer is less than the interest due so the difference is added to the principal. The more you pay, the more you owe.

I remember when the mortgage lender assigned to my branch came to me one day very excited because, as he said, "we now can really compete." He proceeded to explain a new loan program, the negative amortization one. When he finished I told him that I thought that was a travesty and that I did not want him to sell that to any of my customers. He was really upset and went to complain to his boss. His boss complained to my boss and my boss called me and told me to lay off him and that I was not making bank policy and that the bank policy was to make these loans. I do not want to sound like a know-it-all, but the results made me looked like a genius. The bank was declared insolvent by the FDIC and sold to a group of New York investors for almost nothing. All of us who had stock in the bank lost everything and the top executives removed or sidelined. Those were very trying days because our customers were afraid about their deposits even though for the most part all deposits were insured and none of the depositors lost anything.

Bank Atlantic did not go insolvent right away, but eventually they also had to be sold to BB&T bank due to the same problem as Bank United. The government bailed out most of the very large banks, but neglected to help those local medium sized banks with bailout money. The new owners of Bank United kept the same name and as of this writing are still in business. My position was not affected by the change and I was able to even win the third place of a production contest the first year of the new ownership. My studies were going well and I started to work on my dissertation. This is one of the hardest parts of the doctorate program because you have to write a fully documented research study which has to be approved by a panel of three professors every step of the way.

My final dissertation had 156 pages and took me the better part of two years to write it, do the field research, and have it approved by the panel of professors, the head of research, and the dean of business for the University. The title of my dissertation is: "Voluntary Turnover: An Empirical Study of the Factors Influencing the High Turnover of Bank Tellers." The actual field research was done using 6 local banks and more than 300 respondents. The results fully supported my hypothesis that low salary and low organizational commitment were strong indicators of the intention to quit on bank tellers.

One of the hardest requirements of the doctorate program was what they called the Comprehensive Exam. This exam was an all day affair where you are tested in two subjects in the morning and two in the afternoon. The exam could have questions on any topic of the four subjects. The students pick two of the subjects and the other two every student takes. To make things even harder, the test must be done in writing by hand. This was incredible to me. We spent five years taking classes, doing papers, and typing the dissertation using the computer, but the exam was done with pencil and paper. This rule presented an added challenge for me. I have the worst handwriting in the world, or at least in Hialeah. Not only I had to prepare myself by learning the material, but also practicing handwriting so that the graders could actually read and understand what I wrote. I was a nervous wreck for many months prior to the exam because you must pass three of the four subjects and you only had two chances to do it.

The day of the test came and the results were not good for me. I had only passed two of the subjects and I needed to go back in a month and take the other two and pass at least one of them. Needless to say the level of anxiety and fear was getting the best of me. If did not pass at least one, I would not graduate. All the other efforts in the classes and in the dissertation would be useless and all the student loan money that I owed would be for nothing. I worked very hard during that month. I went back the second time and fortunately I passed both subjects and I was ready to graduate after five years of hard work, sacrifice, and tensions. My wife was also happy that it was over because I must have been insufferable during those years and only a "saint" like her could put up with such a test.

My father, who was 88 years old when I started the doctorate program, could not believe his eyes. He used to tell me: "I cannot believe that the worst student of "Colegio Cubano Arturo Montori" is going to get a doctorate degree." Of course my father was always looking for something to joke about and this statement was just a joke, because I know he was very proud of me. One thing I regret is that he died just a few months (January 30, 2009) before my graduation in May 2009. He was 92 when he died. I know that even though he was not at the graduation ceremony in person, I could feel his presence and his smile as I walked across the stage.

Our son Robert and Annie Maresca were married on February 20, 2009. It was a beautiful wedding at Saint David Catholic Church in Davie, Florida. Alexander Marcos Woods, our fifth grandchild was born in July 2009 and our sixth, Sophia Breña Ochoa was born in July 2010.

Chapter Forty Five
What happened after the Doctorate Graduation?
The trip is coming to an end

After my graduation in May 2009 I started to look for a full time teaching position. I secured several part-time teaching jobs. I started again at Miami Dade College and The Center for Financial Training. I got a position at Carlos Albizu University teaching in their Master's program. I applied for a full-time position the first time at Miami Dade College and I was not accepted. I was still working at Bank United mainly because I was making pretty good money and it was hard to break loose. I also applied at several other universities and only got one offer. I could not accept this offer because the salary was not enough. I would have had to quit Bank United and all the other part-time teaching jobs. Because of the changes in the social security rules, I could not get my social security pension until I was 67 years of age. In 2009 I was only 66 so I could not count on that to supplement the salary that the University offered me. I tried to negotiate a temporary or one-time bonus for the first year, but they would not do it.

I applied to many out of state universities and many of them not even sent me a rejection letter. They simply ignored me. I think a lot had to do with the fact that I was still working making a lot of more money than I would be making at a university and for them that did not make sense. If I would have the opportunity of an interview, I would have explained what my plan was. I applied for Miami Dade College again, but I was not hired for a full time position. It was kind of strange that after working there as an adjunct professor for over 20 years, they would not hire me for a full time position, I think the fact that I was still in banking had something to do with it, but maybe my age influenced them as well.

Finally in November 2010 I was able to retire and obtain my social security monthly income. I had also secured a part-time teaching position at South University and at Nova Southeastern University. In both of these I was teaching in their Masters program. I applied for the third time at Miami Dade College and again I was rejected. I was so mad and decided that I was not going to apply ever again. I continued to apply at many universities, but nothing materialized. Because I was still at Bank United and had all these part time teaching jobs, our combined salaries (Yolanda had also retired with social security), 2010 was the year with highest adjusted gross income of our history.

Bank United was getting worse by the minute. The pressure was getting to me and I was feeling sick all the time. The stress was too much to take so in 2011 I decided to quit Bank United and retire from banking after 41 years in the industry. I did not have a full time position, but I figured we could manage until one came along, but I needed to get out of that racket, and I needed to show that I was not working in a bank anymore and that I was able to devote my career to academia in order to eliminate that obstacle. This was a hard decision because I was leaving a large salary plus all the sales incentives, but that was the decision. To also help matters, our youngest son Joey graduated that year from Pennsylvania State University with a doctorate degree in Physics and had obtained a teaching position at a university near Philadelphia. We decided to put our house on the market and downsize to a smaller home where we would not have a mortgage payment to make this drastic change in cash less of a burden.

I tried to get as many classes as I could in all the different places I was teaching and I also found some music jobs along the way. I was told by a coworker at Miami Dade College that they were looking for a full time professor for the Bachelors program at the Wolfson Campus. I told that person that I was not going to apply ever again, but the coworker insisted and told me that this time it might be different. I applied for the fourth time and was accepted and started in August 2013, almost 2 years after I resigned from Bank United. I could finally put my doctorate degree to full use and have a comfortable financial condition. We decided not to sell our home. I am now starting my third year and I like what I do very much.

The story of My Fifty Year Trip ends here, 2012, but I hope the trip continues and we can enjoy our six children and their families. There were some important events that took place while I was finishing the book which I would like to document here. In January 18, 2014 our son Roland married Kristin Bianculli in a ceremony was something we would never forget. Four more grandchildren were born: Giovanni (Gio) William Ochoa on February 2013, Mathew Mario Ochoa on May 2013, Reina Kelley-Rose Ochoa on January 2015, and Juliana Elizabeth Ochoa on January 2016.

I would also like to continue for many more years to teach and help young minds prepare for the business world at Miami Dade College.

278

APPENDIX
PICTURES

Family portrait in 1960 before we our departure from Cuba as political refugees. From left to right: Rolandito, Rubenin, Susana, Rolando, Pepa, Cecilia Lucia, Cecilia, and Pepita

Rolando Ochoa in the height of his TV career

Pepa Berrio my beautiful and talented mother

Family Portrait in front of our house in El Vedado, Havana, Cuba. From left to right: Pepa, Abuelo Manuel, Rolandito, Tavito, Abuela Rita, Rolando, Pepita, Tia Rina, and Tio Octavio

My Great grandmothers: Manuela Muro y Mercedes Pujol

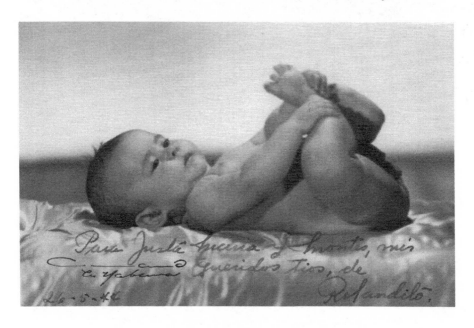

My baby picture

Baby Rolandito with Abuela Coloma Bonnin

Rolandito" OCHOA se desplomó también. Reclinó su cabeza en el hombro de su abuela y esperó durmiendo el resultado del concurso.

CARTELE!

Exhausted Rolandito after a long day with Abuela Rita Garcia

Abuelo Pepe Berrio

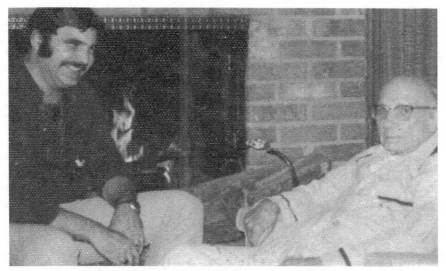

Tavito my cousin and Abuelo Manuel Ochoa

Rolandito's first big success imitating Pedro Infante in
"Mi Chorro de Voz"

Rolandito in the peak of his TV career

Scene from the movie :"Angeles de la Calle" with Emilia Giu and Gustavo Rojo who had the parts of my parents.

Rolandito as the "Mascot" of the Cuban Sugar Kings Triple A baseball team. In the background the great "Cerro" baseball stadium in Havana Cuba

Rolando en Santa Barbara California dreaming of an acting career.

Conjunto Tropical playing at Milander Auditorium in Hialeah Florida.
From left to right: Arnoldo Velazquez, Luis Puga, Rolandito, Willie
Trueba, Frank Sainz, and Pepe Pino

Our wedding picture December 20, 1965 at Saint John Bosco Catholic
Church in Miami, Florida

Our first "home" in Columbia, South Carolina

Pictures during the two years in the U.S. Army

Family Portrait in my parents apartment in Hialeah in 1982.

Picture of the celebration of 25th Wedding Anniversary. From left to right: Robert, Roland, Yolanda Maria, Rolando, Yolanda, Maria Teresa, Will, and Joey.

Tete, my mother-in-law, with us for her 80th birthday. From left to right: Joey, Yolanda Maria, Yolanda, Robert, Tete, Rolando, Maria Teresa, and will. Roland was not in town.

My father Rolando Ochoa in his 90th birthday with my sisters Susana and Pepita with me in the middle

Doctorate graduation picture with Yolanda and Susana May 2009

The six "children" in 2010.

Made in the USA
Columbia, SC
29 August 2017